★ ★ ★ ★ ★ ★

KNOWLEDGE REVOLUTION

FOR ALL AMERICANS

Winning The War Against Ignorance: Empowering Public Schools

★ ★ ★ ★ ★ ★ ★ ★ ★

The Knowledge Network for All Americans is an independent, private, non-profit corporation advocating the creation of responsible learning cultures. The Network disseminates findings to its participants. Individuals or organizations concerned about educational reform are invited to participate in the Knowledge Network.

To order this report, or for further information on how you can participate in the Knowledge Network, call 1-800-736-4877.

Knowledge Network for All Americans
Partners Creating Responsible Learning Cultures
Executive Offices: (703) 522-3535 Fax (703) 522-4143
Knowledge Network Automated Help Line: 1-800-736-4877

Library of Congress Catalog Card Number:
ISBN 0-9634636-0-8

Open letter to Parents, 1992 Presidential Candidates and Members of Congress, Governors and Legislators, Educators and Employers, Media and Community Leaders—All Americans:

We are giving away the American Dream. Most Americans, especially the disadvantaged, have no ownership of the Dream. Over the past decade, 60 percent of *all* Americans lost income because of their inadequate skills and productivity. *This giveaway is leading to national frustration and anger.*

We celebrate the success of our hi-tech military power, while other countries become more economically productive. We consume more, but save and invest less. Other nations recognize that tomorrow's competitive edge is forged in today's crucible of human and physical resource development. Under a U.S. military security umbrella, many foreign countries are preparing better-educated, more-productive and better-paid workers than the United States.

Compared with other modern nations, we face declining academic achievement, lower-skilled and lower-paid jobs and a dropping standard of living for our families. We are mortgaging, not investing, in our future. American students, workers and managers are failing to master the knowledge and skills necessary to build successful, satisfying lives. *Consequently, Americans born in the 1960s and 1970s are the first generation to experience a standard of living lower than that of their parents.*

Competitiveness in our global knowledge economy requires focusing on the public schools because they educate 90 percent of the American people. We have nine million young children in preschool or day care. We have 42 million students in 83,500 public elementary and secondary schools. They cannot, and must not, wait until the year 2000 for our schools to improve. We have 14 million students in postsecondary education. We have 126 million workers who need education and training to become more skilled and more productive! Yet the purpose of education is greater than this. America's children and adults must become educationally competitive to enjoy an improved quality of life tomorrow. Our entire democratic society depends upon citizens educated to participate in important issues of public policy.

The prophetic 1983 report, *A Nation At Risk,* warned of the growing national crisis in education. Many courageous reformers have labored since then without widespread or lasting success. While much can be learned from them, we can no longer wait for gradual education reform. *Knowledge Revolution for All Americans: Winning the War Against Ignorance—Empowering Public Schools* is taken from a major study that presents a comprehensive strategy to overcome our nation-threatening challenge.[1] As signers of this open letter to the American people, we individually or as a group do not necessarily endorse all findings or recommendations contained in this handbook. We do agree that readers should carefully consider this report and select those action steps that are most appropriate for them. This report calls on all Americans to become aggressive Knowledge Revolutionaries. We must debate findings and recommendations, take responsibility, demand action and reclaim our future—for our nation, ourselves, our children and our grandchildren—before it is too late!

Terrel H. Bell
U.S. Secretary of Education, 1981–1984

William Verity
U.S. Secretary of Commerce, 1987–1989
Chairman, U.S. Chamber of Commerce, 1980–1981

Thomas Boysen
Commissioner, Kentucky Department of Education

Stuart Gothold
Superintendent of Schools
Los Angeles County

Floretta McKenzie
Superintendent of Schools, Washington, D.C., 1981–1988

Augustus F. Hawkins
U.S. House of Representatives
Chairman, Education & Labor Committee, 1984–1990

Bruce Christensen
President & CEO,
Public Broadcasting Service

Ramon Cortines
Superintendent, San Francisco Schools, 1986–1992

Kent Lloyd
President, Knowledge For All Americans Center

Vincent Reed
Vice President, Education/ Communication
The Washington Post

KNOWLEDGE REVOLUTION FOR ALL AMERICANS

Winning The War Against Ignorance: Empowering Public Schools

APPENDICES

INTRODUCTION

The greatest leadership failure in American history is taking place before our eyes. We confront individual and national disaster despite our past leadership in education, training, research, innovation, technology, entrepreneurship and management. Without dramatic action, two out of three of our children will be taken hostage in a losing war against ignorance. The myth that this war can be won by public schools alone is a cruel public joke reflecting a default in community and national leadership.

Throughout American history, every national crisis has required dynamic leadership on all levels to challenge citizens to put aside private interests in favor of public interest. In the 20th century, we have united to defend political freedom against totalitarian dictatorships around the world. We have united to create economic prosperity for our families and neighbors. With scientific knowledge and space technology, we have united to place the first man on the moon.

Several forces undermine courageous efforts to become educationally competitive. *First*, the culture shock of today's global knowledge economy is jolting the world. *Second*, this generation has lost its understanding of and commitment to personal and civic responsibilities essential to America and its international leadership. *Third*, our nation's institutions and public schools are failing to educate most students with knowledge sufficient to earn a decent living in a world of accelerating change. *Fourth*, America's culture of immediate gratification is exploiting children and adolescents. These factors have produced a generation of Americans relatively ignorant by today's demands.

Relevant knowledge is information understood, translated through a useful value framework, and skillfully applied to meeting a challenge. All Americans need relevant knowledge to succeed as students, parents, citizens, consumers and workers in our global knowledge society.

We must invest ourselves in developing responsible learning cultures in every organization—family, school, business, media, community and government—to fight the cancer of ignorance spreading over our country. Competitiveness in our global knowledge economy requires focusing on the public schools because they educate 90 percent of the American people. New investment incentives for public schools, however, must be tied to educational reform and improved student performance. *Before we waste another generation, we must undertake a Third American Revolution—a Knowledge Revolution for All Americans.*

NON-COMPETITIVE AMERICANS[2]

Losing the War Against Ignorance

We are losing the war against ignorance through our faltering institutions—families, schools, communities, corporations, media and governments. *Only one of two American youths between the ages of 17 and 21 is now developing the knowledge to succeed in college, hold a productive job, and participate responsibly as a citizen, parent or consumer.*

In 1983, the National Commission on Excellence in Education gave a prophetic warning: "Our nation is at risk. Our once unchallenged preeminence ... is being overtaken by competitors throughout the world ... the educational foundations of our society are presently being eroded by a rising tide of mediocrity that threatens our very future as a nation and a people. What was unimaginable a generation ago has begun to occur—others are matching and surpassing our educational attainments."

By our failure to invest in people, we have sacrificed one generation of American citizens and are now risking a second. Academic achievement of students in the 1990s is no better than it was in the early 1970s. The National Assessment of Educational Progress (NAEP) reports consistently poor performance by American students, when compared with other students in modern nations, in mathematics, science, geography, history, civics, literature, writing skills and the arts. This is not too surprising when the United States provides only 180 school days per year compared with England's 192, Germany's 210 and Japan's 243 days.[3] American students are learning facts and information, but are unable to comprehend meaning. *Our schools are failing to educate children to become responsible, knowledgeable adults!*

Most young people find a difficult transition from high

school to work or college. Today, both high school dropouts and graduates have decreased skill levels, reduced productivity and a lower standard of living—condemning them to lives of borderline poverty. School dropouts seriously erode the nation's economic competitiveness. In 1991, unemployment rates for teenagers averaged around 16.4 percent for whites, 22.9 percent for Hispanics, and 36.3 percent for African Americans. The 1981 high school class dropouts have collectively lost $228 billion in personal income and cost the nation $68 billion in taxes.

Prospects for high school graduates are not much better. *A high school diploma is not sufficient preparation to support a family in the global knowledge economy.* In 1973, 60 percent of young men under age 24 were earning enough to support a family of three above the poverty level. By 1990, only 34 percent could do the same. Real entry wages paid in 1991 to male high school graduates were 26.5 percent lower than their counterparts received in 1979. Entry-level pay for college graduates declined by 9.8 percent during these years.[4]

Almost four million adult Americans cannot read, sign their names, or perform simple addition and subtraction. *Thirty million workers can read and write only minimally, and another 40 million lack the basic skills to get by in a technological and rapidly changing world. The United States ranks 49th in literacy among 158 members of the United Nations.* Illiteracy and crimes are correlated. Some 85 percent of juvenile delinquents have inadequate reading skills; 75 percent of prison inmates are functionally illiterate. Illiteracy and poverty also are closely associated. Teenagers with poor basic academic skills are four times more likely to live in poverty than teenagers with good skills.

Illiteracy costs over $200 billion annually in welfare payments, crime, job incompetence, lost tax revenues and remedial education. Because many people have not learned to keep commitments or behave responsibly, the costs of risk management have skyrocketed—security personnel, surveillance technology and legal work. *Scarce national resources are being drained to support our uneducated, unskilled, unproductive and dissatisfied citizens who are "ignorant" by standards of a global knowledge culture.*

For decades, our European and Asian competitors have required high standards for all high school graduates. We have not! They have motivated students to excel in school by making a clear connection between school curriculum, personal life and job requirements. We have not! They have defined educational success as the ability to demonstrate competitive knowledge. We have not! They have invested heavily in training and technology and demanded high-level skills and productivity. We have not!

Losing America's Civic Heritage

Since World War II, America's civic culture has withered through benign neglect and unwise choices of citizens and leaders alike. The Founding Fathers established checks and balances of constitutional power to protect the "public good." Nevertheless, civic culture over the past 40 years has been undermined by the corrupting influence of special interest groups.[5] We have accumulated a massive national debt of $4 trillion.

Since 1950, federal spending has grown faster than productivity. *Powerful special interest groups have exploited public resources. In the past 15 years, social security, health and medicare costs increased drastically, while education funding fell in constant dollars.*[6] *The United States now spends one-third more to service the federal debt than it spends on all its public schools. In 1992, 74 percent of the federal budget expenditures went for military-industrial activities (24 percent) and civilian entitlements (50 percent).* It is difficult to hold political leaders accountable for conspiring with special interests. For most of the past four decades, the federal government has been stalled, divided between a Republican president and a Democratic Congress.

Our civic culture was shaped by spokesmen of America's political revolution, who declared that "all men are created equal, that they are endowed by their Creator with certain unalienable rights, that among these are life, liberty and the pursuit of happiness." Following a courageous revolutionary war, early patriots negotiated a new constitution that begins:

"We the people of the United States, in order to form a more perfect union, establish justice, insure domestic tranquility, provide for the common defense, promote the general welfare, and secure the blessings of liberty to ourselves and our posterity, do ordain and establish this Constitution for the United States of America."

The building of a nation would depend on an *educated citizenry's* personal and civic morality, knowledge and common agreement. John Adams said, "Liberty cannot be preserved without a general knowledge among the people." Thomas Jefferson stated, "If a nation expects to be ignorant and free it expects what never was and never will be." Character values and civic responsibilities were to be learned before leaving childhood and entering responsible adulthood. The mission of family, church and school was to promote personal virtue or character education to balance self-interest and public interest. As the new constitution was ratified in 1788, the Congress declared, "*Religion, morality and knowledge being necessary to good government and the happiness of mankind, schools and the means of education shall forever be encouraged.*"[7]

All American citizens were expected to rise above their "natural vices" through religious instruction, education and experience to become responsible—contributing and accountable—members of family and community. The community in turn would establish a representative government to balance liberty and authority in carrying out rules for living together with peace, justice and prosperity. Citizens would give their consent to be governed by laws in exchange for protection of self, family and property. Jefferson saw the "art of government" as being honest, while Madison held "the end of government" as justice. Implied political "contracts" between responsible citizens and leaders would legitimate constitutional governments. When governments no longer kept their contracts, they would be changed by election or, if necessary, community resistance.

The working principles of America's experiment in democracy were taken seriously, openly debated and adapted to practical living by civic leaders and ordinary citizens. Values of human and property rights, diversity, privacy, freedom, and due process were "rights" of the individual. Values of justice, equality, honesty, authority, participation and patriotism were "obligations" of citizenship. These national civic values, however, have not always been supported. Not until a painful civil rights movement did the nation finally recognize the constitutionally protected rights of all citizens regardless of race, color, creed, ethnicity, gender, age or disability.

America's Economic Revolution

In their lifetime, older Americans have seen their individual, family and community lifestyles redefined by successive economic cultures. America has moved from the agrarian economy of the early 1900s to the industrial economy of the 1950s, to the service information economy of the 1990s. In the agricultural economy, life revolved around the land and the large intergenerational families that worked it. Most farm laborers were relatively unskilled or semiskilled. Small businesses provided support services; the few large businesses provided equipment. The school day and school year were structured around early morning and evening farm chores, spring planting and summer harvesting. In the one-room schoolhouse, basic reading, writing and arithmetic were available for children during late fall, winter and early spring. High school graduation was unusual for men and a luxury for most women. The transition from the local agricultural economy to the national industrial economy occurred in conjunction with the Great Depression.

During and after World War II, large-scale manufacturing employed a majority of workers. Mass-produced goods and services shaped the lifestyles of most American families. Productive agricultural corporations eliminated the need for most farmers. Men began to work away from the home—10 hours or more per day, five or six days of the week. The traditional family and its pattern of child rearing began to change. Returning veterans bought homes with government-guaranteed loans, attended college on the GI Bill and traveled the 25,000 miles of "national security highways." They became semiskilled, blue-collar and technical workers, or managers and professionals in "gray flannel suits."

The industrial economy gave rise to the modern corporation with its large capital assets, such as plants, equipment and inventories. These corporations had the capacity to attract venture and investment capital with limited personal risk. By the 1950s, the top 500 national corporations produced half of the nation's industrial output, owned 75 percent of the nation's industrial assets and 40 percent of the nation's corporate profits. In response to the Cold War, massive federal funds were channeled into defense industries. A new generation of highly productive, prosperous workers and consumers demanded new manufactured goods and services. Business developed marketing, advertising, sales and distribution systems to meet and stimulate the demand. Between 1950 and 1980, a surprising 80 percent of the nation was classified as middle class, with only 10 percent as poor and 10 percent as rich.

During this period, most mothers raised children and became household managers. They provided personal support services for husbands who were working or children who were attending school. Public schools, which gradually displaced parents in the occupational training of children, reflected the high-volume, standardized production model of industry. Children moved from grade to grade through a planned sequence of standard subjects. Most were taught with emphasis on facts, information and standardized tests. Only about half of all students graduated. Well-paying factory jobs awaited graduates and non-graduates alike. The top 15 percent of students went on to attend four-year colleges and universities. Those who graduated took management positions in expanding corporate and government bureaucracies.

Culture Shock: Competing In Our Global Knowledge Economy

By the last quarter of the 20th century, foreign competitors began seizing traditional U.S. markets—at home and abroad—by producing better products at lower prices. Employment opportunities in America's "rust belt" industries began to decline. Between 1975 and 1990, our 500 largest industrial companies created no additional jobs and represented only 10 percent of the civilian workforce. Since 1973, America's standard of living has averaged less than one-half the growth of the preceding 25 years, resulting in a total loss of $28,000 for each person. *By the year 2000, semiskilled, blue-collar manufacturing workers will number only 10 percent of the American labor force.* As both agricultural and manufacturing jobs dwindled, two new types of service jobs developed—stagnant labor-intensive personal services and highly productive information services.

Over the last two decades, the profile of the American workforce also changed dramatically. Women joined the paid workforce in greater numbers than ever before. To maintain their lifestyles, both men and women worked longer hours and more days each year. With both mother and father absent from the household during the day, quality child care was needed by most young families. Today, we have a child-care crisis.[8] Schools and teachers are burdened with greater responsibilities for the care and development of children. They are constrained by an outdated, ineffective industrial model of education.

The daily life of each American is being rapidly transformed by a highly specialized, information-based, global knowledge economy.[9] Today 80 percent of our goods and services face international competition. *Knowledge has become the power that drives productivity in advanced competitive nations.* Knowledge is the critical input, investment and service. Knowledge provides the livelihood of the largest workforce of professional, managerial and technical people ever employed in the U.S. and other modern nations. *In the last 30 years, information workers grew from 42 to almost 60 percent of the workforce. Of the new jobs created between 1988 and 2000, 54 percent will be in knowledge-based services.* Knowledge also drives hi-tech agriculture and manufacturing. The fastest growing occupations in the 1990s will require employees with higher math, language and reasoning capabilities than most students now achieve.

These occupations also bring higher pay. Education is the principal investment toward earning. A higher level of education brings greater entry pay, income growth and stability of employment. College graduates 25 to 29 years old earn 43 percent more than same-age high school graduates, and those 30 to 34 years old earn 57 percent more. Moreover, while pay for college graduates has been rising, the real earnings of high school dropouts and even of high school graduates has been declining. Nearly one-third of dropouts are unemployed, and more than one-fifth of families headed by a high school dropout live in poverty.

Often the knowledge worker's high-value product is not tangible. Today, an organization's technological progress increases as its number of "information translators" increases. *Most American students and workers are not being educated with the knowledge and skills necessary to be competitive. They will become casualties in an undeclared war against ignorance. By contrast, our top global competitors are nations with the strongest public education systems.* They invest in developing knowledge workers—tomorrow's vital resource. Meanwhile, in America, continued belief in eight crippling myths holds U.S. citizens in bondage.

AMERICANS HELD HOSTAGE: Cultural Myths Examined

MYTH #1: Most American families have healthy, well-behaved, smart children.

Families in the United States provide the critical foundation for each individual's development. The contemporary structure of this "institution" varies widely from two-parent, single-parent, and stepfamilies to adoptive and foster families. While there are many outstanding exceptions, most families are inadequately preparing children for the demands of today's world.

FINDING A: *Many children in America are not born healthy, do not receive adequate nutrition, do not live in safe homes and neighborhoods, and do not get preventive health care, therefore experiencing impaired educational development.*

Children without health insurance use fewer medical services than those with coverage. Most poor and minority children have more health problems because they lack adequate health insurance protection.

- Some 8.3 million children under age 18 have no health insurance.
- Twenty percent of our population is covered by public health insurance as compared to over 90 percent in European countries.
- The U.S. has the highest mortality rate for infants and for children under the age of five among industrial nations.
- The U.S. leads in deaths by preventable causes for children under five, such as fire and homicide.

- American children have considerably lower immunization rates for polio, mumps, measles and rubella.
- The growing epidemic of alcohol and illegal drug use by pregnant women, and the associated rising rates of HIV infection, threaten the health and development of 375,000 babies annually.[10]
- One in five American children between ages 3 and 17 experiences developmental delays, behavioral problems, or learning disabilities from illnesses often preventable with good nutrition or treatable with antibiotics. Children from single-parent families are two to three times more likely to suffer these problems than children in two-parent homes.

The emotional health of American children has deteriorated over the past generation. Many mothers and fathers are too stressed and drained emotionally by job demands to properly nurture their children. The failure to develop close, enduring bonds can have devastating consequences for children.

- After homicides and motor vehicle accidents, which are often alcohol related, suicide is the third-leading cause of death among adolescents.[11]
- Half of all young people in middle school abuse drugs or alcohol; each day over 500 begin to use illegal drugs and 1,000 start to drink alcoholic beverages.[12]
- Fifteen percent of children suffer mental disorders, such as depression, anxiety, attention deficit and hyperactivity, and of those, only 10 percent receive treatment.

FINDING B: *Most parents are not providing their children with character education that encourages responsible, constructive behavior.*

Parents influence children's moral development by the example they set in their own daily lives. Most American children of every age, race and income group do not receive the necessary nurturing and discipline that provide motivation and structure for constructive moral and cognitive development. In the past two decades, social and economic changes have altered family roles, relationships and routines. Most parents do not regularly share household responsibilities with their children. By not contributing to the family, children are unable to develop feelings of satisfaction, pride, and "ownership." Through over-indulging and over-directing their children, parents unintentionally foster destructive dependence. Half of all children will live in a one-parent household at some time during their school years. More children are growing up without a father in the home, which particularly impacts the socialization of boys. On average, employed adults are working longer hours and more days.[13] Even when both parents are in the home, they often do not take the time or energy to instill moral values in their children.

FINDING C: *Far too many children enter school unprepared to learn and can leave high school without the basic knowledge and skills to get decent jobs or to enter college.*

Most parents are not systematically preparing children with the learning attitudes and skills necessary for success in school, such as enjoyment of reading, opportunities for self-expression, and completion of tasks.[14] Television is frequently used as a convenient babysitter. From this passive form of entertainment, children tend to develop the attitude that only if learning is easy and entertaining will they make the effort.

- Each week, the average working parent spends about 30 minutes in conversation with his/her children, while most of these children watch nearly 30 hours of television.
- Forty-two percent of high school seniors score below functional or intermediate proficiency in reading, with writing achievement levels at "minimal" to "adequate."
- American students score below the international average in all areas of math.
- America's advanced science students rank last in biology, third from the bottom in physics, and next to last in chemistry among students in 12 countries.[15]

FINDING D: *Most self-reliant, academically achieving, well-rounded and healthy children have parents who have created a stable, supportive family.*[16]

Healthy, strong or excellent families include both two-parent and single-parent households, although the latter are more vulnerable to environmental demands. Strong families are developed by working at it—consistently improving and building on strengths. They share common characteristics that cut across all ethnic and socioeconomic backgrounds: full commitment, unconditional love, consistent training or discipline, good communication, high expectations, basic moral and civic values, time together, shared traditions, spiritual core, problem-solving skills and participative decision making.

MYTH #2: Media programming and advertising are harmless for our children.

Mass media in the United States are a major influence in each American's life. They include public and private network television, cable channels, records and tapes, newspapers, specialty newsletters, magazines and books. While there are many notable exceptions, most mass media are not adequately reporting the progress in public school reform, or worse, they are undermining responsible learning cultures.

FINDING A: *Most electronic mass media—a dominant force that can mask our failures—are rapidly transforming millions of Americans into relatively ignorant and exploited people.*[17]

Formal schooling competes poorly with the culture of immediate gratification, which is portrayed dramatically to adolescents every day. The popular culture communicates with nearly every home, work and leisure place. Television and video viewing is associated with a shrinking written vocabulary.

- In 1945, the average 6- to 14-year-old American child used 25,000 words as compared to 10,000 today.
- Excessive television watching distorts the learning process, reduces reading and contributes to illiteracy.

FINDING B: *Advertising seriously undermines constructive values, attitudes and behavior of American children.*

Advertisers carefully target their audiences to the sale of

goods and services. Because effective advertising can earn huge profits, media messages to young people have increased dramatically.

- In 1991, corporations spent $130 billion on advertising, 50 percent more per capita than is spent in any other nation. They targeted about $500 million to reach children, five times what they spent a decade earlier. Children ages 4 to 12 indirectly influence household budgets by an $8 billion expenditure annually.
- The television industry would lose $250 million annually in advertising revenue if the audience were to shrink by 1 percent.
- The lucrative television-toy linkup has created a "need" in children to have certain toys, as well as fast foods, breakfast cereals and athletic shoes.
- Businesses sell to a growing audience of young adults, 60 percent of whom do not read books. They also sell to the average "postadolescent," who spends 40 hours and at least $30 a week being entertained by non-print media.

Television shapes values, attitudes and behavior when it conveys pleasure-seeking and immediate gratification. Sex, drugs, alcohol, violence, wealth and materialism are glamorized. Sex is commercialized, depersonalized and separated from emotional involvement and commitment. Advertisers use sexually irresponsible messages to sell entertainment and merchandise to younger and younger audiences. Also the United States has the highest teen pregnancy rate in the industrialized world.

- One out of 10 girls aged 15 to 19 gets pregnant each year; two-thirds of them are unmarried.[18]
- Of the estimated 12 million cases of sexually transmitted diseases, 85 percent occur among teenagers and young adults.[19]

Cues about alcohol and drugs bombard our everyday life. We receive a constant stream of messages about the thrill of getting high and feeling good. Young people who abuse drugs are likely to drop out of school, to engage in premature and unprotected sexual activity and to commit crimes.

- The alcohol industry alone spends over $1 billion a year to advertise its products.[20]
- Some alcoholic beverage companies even underwrite concert tours directed at teens and preteens.

The United States has the second highest rate of cigarette consumption in the industrialized world.

- Lung cancer caused approximately 143,000 American deaths in 1991.
- A company's use of cartoon characters in cigarette ads increased its brand's popularity with juveniles 12 to 17 years old.
- A tobacco company donated $17 million in 1991 to schools, hospitals, cultural and charity groups, targeting minority organizations and legislators who might help defeat tobacco tax and antismoking bills.

The pop culture as promoted by mass media transforms moderation into excess, freedom into chaos, humility into arrogance, courage into abandon, integrity into deceit, justice into oppression, industry into sloth, generosity into greed, cooperation into conflict, optimism into nihilism, and community into narcissism. The pop culture distorts who we are and who we should be. It undermines our ability to deal constructively with the demands of our environment, leading to avoidance of life's challenges. It rejects authority, resisting any attempt to hold behavior to a set of standards. *America's culture of immediate gratification is sapping our resources, exploiting our citizens and creating a growing amoral, uneducated, unhealthy and unemployable underclass of Americans.*

FINDING C: *The link between media violence and increasingly violent social behavior is well documented.*

"After months of stormy protests over the heavy metal song 'Cop Killer,' rapper Ice-T and record producer Time Warner Inc. agreed today to stop selling the song. In an unusual move, the company said it would recall copies of the modest-selling album 'Body Count,' containing the song that has become a major point of contention with police groups and conservative organizations across the country. The song has also prompted a boycott of Time Warner and threats to sue company officers and directors on behalf of police officers killed in the line of duty."[21]

Exposure to violence has a desensitizing and cumulative effect on children that carries over into adulthood. The viewing of television violence affects normal child development, increasing levels of physical aggressiveness and violence.[22] Children are unable to distinguish between fantasy and reality in their early years. They are exposed to the idealization of violence, associating it with love and goodness as well as with hate and hostility. Heroes who solve problems with violent action are presented as role models. As youth are exposed to more violence in the media, their participation in violent crimes increases. Younger children are committing more serious and violent crimes today.

- The U.S. murder rate doubled between 1945 and 1974.
- In 1991, there were 23,000 murders in America, a record high—almost 15 times higher than in Japan.[23]
- Gunshot wounds are the leading cause of death among teenage boys ages 15 to 19.

FINDING D: *Mass media have failed to report, or have distorted, the public education story.*

Most media representatives neglect serious reporting and commentary on public education. They are not literate about education as a complex institution in American life and how it relates to economics or the civic culture. The activities of education—one of the nation's largest industries—are not being reported by the media to parents and taxpayers.[24]

- Only about a dozen of 3,500 network employees in both print and broadcast media work on education full time.
- A study of air time for a 30-month period showed that only 350 of the 36,000 pieces (.9 percent) on all subjects were devoted to education stories. Approximately 150 of these pieces had little to do with schools directly.

FINDING E: *Public Broadcasting Service (PBS) represents a positive example of educational TV Programming.*

While major TV networks show two or three hours each of "back to school" specials, PBS and its member stations air 15 hours of education-related programming during the first week of September. PBS has daily series for preschoolers and older children, such as *Sesame Street* and *Mr. Rogers*, as well as weekly series on the arts, science and literacy. Primetime shows, such as *Math: Who Needs It?*, focus on education issues throughout the year. Public TV distributes more than 2,000 hours of instructional television (ITV) programming annually, specifically for classroom use, reaching 29 million K–12 students. This year, it enrolls its two-millionth student in TV courses for college credit.

MYTH #3: Working alone, America's public schools can prepare all students for successful futures.

Among the 83,500 public schools in the United States, very few are preparing students with the relevant knowledge to compete successfully in today's global knowledge economy.

FINDING A: *Most students and their parents, as compared to employers and educators, hold starkly different views on America's educational system and how it prepares graduates for adult life.*

A 1991 Harris Poll surveyed a large sample of employers, college and vocational school educators, students, parents and the general public. On average, there was a 35 to 40 percent difference between the positive perceptions of students and their parents and the negative perceptions of employers and educators. Parents and students felt very positive about their work and college preparation. Those who employ or educate young high school graduates view the preparation by public schools as "inadequate." The poll cautioned, "*The reality gap is striking and alarming.... The current crop of students and their parents are deluding themselves. Until this gap is closed, little progress can be made in ensuring that America has a truly educated workforce.*"[25]

FINDING B: *American students are not learning responsible citizenship for the classroom, school and society.*

School curriculum seldom includes careful instruction to reinforce basic moral values, such as responsibility, honesty, discipline and mutual respect.[26] Without the civilizing influence of these values, violence in our society, even in our schools, is escalating. Many teachers and students work in unsafe and disruptive environments. The confusion between authoritarianism and legitimate authority is contributing to students' disrespect of teachers and disregard of instruction.

FINDING C: *The traditional "culture of teaching" emphasizes the transmission of information not the development of relevant knowledge.*

The culture of teaching "is powerful enough to undermine other reform efforts because it determines the way pupils spend their time, the nature of the behaviors they practice, and the basis of their self-concepts as learners."[27] Most teachers primarily use lectures and textbook assignments to transfer information. Their core teaching involves giving facts and directions; asking questions; making, monitoring and reviewing assignments; giving and reviewing tests; assigning and reviewing homework; settling disputes and punishing students; marking papers and giving grades. Students are unable to convert information into useful relevant knowledge without skillfully applying it mentally, morally and experientially.

FINDING D: *All American students do not receive equivalent resources—adequate buildings, competent teachers, current books and modern technology.*

Funding inequalities between school districts and states are increasing each year. Most urban and rural disadvantaged children attend impoverished schools. The critical problems in America's inner-city schools—drugs, crime, violence and other social ills—are exacerbated by insufficient funding. The difficult teaching environment has led to teacher shortages and to hiring teachers without necessary training, experience, skills or motivation. These schools often lack the necessary staff and facilities to have libraries, teach science or offer art and music classes. In some cases, financial pressures have forced school districts to tolerate a high level of truancy because they lack desks, chairs or classroom space to serve the children enrolled. Inner-city students often attend school in dirty, crumbling buildings, with inadequate heating, plumbing and broken windows.

- In the 1988–1989 school year, New Jersey's funding ranged from $7,725 per pupil in the Princeton district to $3,538 in the Camden district.[28]
- In 1991, expenditures per pupil nationwide varied from $3,100 per student in Idaho, Mississippi and Utah to over $8,000 in Alaska and New York.[29]

FINDING E: *American students are not well-prepared with the knowledge and career skills necessary for a satisfying and productive future.*

Despite the increasing educational demands of a global knowledge economy, *the National Assessment of Educational Progress (NAEP) reports consistently poor performance by students in all subjects.* Without basic academic and career skills, most young people will experience unemployment and poverty.[30]

- Teenagers lacking these skills are four times more likely to live in poverty.
- Sixty percent of teenage mothers have not completed high school.
- Between 1975 and 1990, the average earnings in constant dollars of 18- to 24-year-olds without high school diplomas fell from $17,543 to $14,075, while the earnings of those with only high school diplomas fell from $20,003 to $15,829.
- Of those who headed households, the rate of incomes below the poverty level nearly doubled by 1990, reaching 34.7 percent (2.7 million households).
- Employers pay an estimated $30 billion annually on formal and informal training, remediation and lost productivity because youth are unprepared to join the workforce.

FINDING F: *Most educators are not organizing and managing effective schools and classrooms.*

Most schools across the nation are not organized to be effective learning centers. Our children are not being prepared for the escalating demands of today's world. Outstanding schools share common characteristics: student-centered, high expectations, orderly, optimistic, purposeful and efficient. *The key factor in effective schools is principal and teacher leadership.* Effective principals and teachers have a clear vision of what their school and classroom could be. They convey that vision to students and parents, negotiating a shared school culture. They communicate their expectations, work collaboratively with students and parents toward goals, provide resources, use participative decision making, enforce reasonable discipline, evaluate student achievement and account for results.

MYTH #4: Higher education need not be part of national public school reform.

Public and private higher education is a major comparative advantage of the United States. Higher education includes community college, four-year college, university, professional and graduate schools. While there are major exceptions, most universities are not influential in public school reform.

FINDING A: *Higher education is a major stakeholder in elementary and secondary school education, the foundation of America's competitiveness in the global knowledge economy.*

Higher education develops human resources critical to a competitive workforce and a well-functioning society, building on the base provided by elementary and secondary schooling. Higher education is in a strategic position to help Americans adapt to the changing demands of our global knowledge economy. It is also the primary vehicle of social mobility for Americans, particularly our growing minority populations.

American higher education generates knowledge and educates knowledge workers. It leads the world in research, institutional strength, curricular diversity, educational opportunities and international knowledge. In addition to nearly 14 million Americans, it currently enrolls 400,000 foreign students, who provide $4 billion in foreign exchange earnings to the United States.

Higher education also prepares teachers for our nation's school systems.[31] Schools of education on most campuses, however, accept students with lower grades. Typically, they provide weak teacher preparation. Education students usually pay the same as those in other fields, even though their education costs less to provide. In effect, their tuition subsidizes those who benefit from strong research departments and professional schools.

State universities, as recipients of public money, are responsible for educating the majority of teachers. Yet these universities face increased funding competition for scarce public revenues from K–12 education and other public services. Their budgets have been reduced by legislators who see higher education making little contribution to improvement of elementary and secondary education.

Teachers in elementary, middle and high school help students lay the foundation of knowledge and skills necessary for adulthood, including academic performance in college. Because so many students are poorly prepared by our education systems, higher education and employers are forced to provide remedial training. The contributions of higher education to school reform have been deficient in vision, advocacy and leadership, even though higher education will benefit directly from reform of public education. Pioneering programs for widespread school reform, however, are underway: the Coalition of Essential Schools (Brown University); the Accelerated Schools Project (Stanford University); the School Development Program (Yale University).

FINDING B: *Because the humanities no longer play a central role in higher education, the teaching of personal and civic values, so critical to community development and the global knowledge society, is weakened.*

In the last century, character education was central to university training. Clear civic values—community, discipline, creativity, achievement and tolerance—were taught as a part of the humanities. These values influenced the moral, social and academic development of teachers and students. Yet the connection between higher education's classic value base and general and teacher education has been weakened, negatively affecting learning, morale and performance of students, graduates and professors.

Today, most colleges and universities do not focus on the vital importance of the humanities, which are basic to our cultural heritage and to understanding our global partners. Humanities education stresses shared cultural understandings and appreciation of individual differences. Both are essential to the communication and cooperation needed to integrate and improve society and work in the global knowledge economy.[32]

FINDING C: *Higher education can improve elementary and secondary education by reforming itself, which includes raising admission standards.*

Pressure is growing to reform undergraduate education, particularly teacher education. Both the higher education and public school reform movements are concerned about content, teaching and student achievement. Many educators within the higher education community are calling for renewing core curricula, increasing international content and using integrative, interdisciplinary approaches. They point to the need for teaching critical thinking, involving students more actively in classroom learning and linking curriculum content to workplace and community through experiential learning.

Higher education has become fragmented into specialized disciplines with curricular options for distinctive career tracks. Disciplines are narrowly focused and lack research budgets to support work that is broadly integrative, policy-relevant, or applied to practical problems of educational or economic productivity.

Colleges and universities can begin to reform by raising admissions standards, which tell high school graduates what they need to know. Higher education faculty can write more thought-provoking public school textbooks and create tools to assess learning. Agencies that accredit institutions of higher learning can focus more on assessing outputs of student learning than on an institution's inputs of library resources and faculty credentials.

As state budget crises over scarce resources focus attention on accountability, *higher education will be held accountable for its performance in exchange for public and private funding.* Reform of higher education will have spill-over effects for elementary and secondary education, just as significant contributions to public school reform will stimulate higher education reform.

MYTH #5: Community organizations have little influence on today's children.

Historically, voluntary community organizations have served as essential support groups for socializing children and supporting primary and secondary schools in neighborhoods. Today, families and public schools have an even greater need for this support network. *Although illustrative only, this section describes six community organizations that are having remarkable influence on children and schools. These examples offer evidence that community leadership can make a significant difference in children's lives.*

FINDING A: *Newspapers can develop community programs to improve school learning and can recognize parents, teachers and principals for their contribution to public schools.*

The Washington Post, for example, has an educational services program headed by Vice President/Communications Vincent Reed, former U.S. Department of Education Assistant Secretary of Elementary and Secondary Education. The mulitfaceted program focuses the *Post*'s resources on aiding education, primarily public education in the Washington, D.C. area. "Inside the Washington Post" is a classroom program that helps teachers reinforce those fundamental skills that students must master to meet mandated academic objectives. "Learning Partners" encourages parents to work with their children using the newspaper to raise self esteem and to reinforce academic skills. The *Post* also has community awards programs that recognize excellent teachers and principals.

FINDING B: *Low-rent housing developers create incentive programs to support inner-city public schools.*

In Los Angeles, EXXCEL provides a rental discount of up to $140 per month to 43 inner-city families if a parent's child does well in school and participates in extra learning activities. Tenants' children have access to study rooms, textbooks, computers, reference materials, tutors and parent volunteers. Good grades earn students cash, tickets to movies, or trips to Disneyland. If students meet minimum college entrance requirements by the time they graduate from high school, they earn scholarships to cooperating colleges and universities. University graduate students in education, family counseling or psychology who also live in the housing complex get rent discounts for their work as tutors and counselors. Working together, parents, students, local principals, graduate students and university officials are demonstrating that a community-based educational support system can provide incentives for raising the performance of disadvantaged students.[33]

FINDING C: *The Girls Scouts Organization helps girls to become confident, capable young women who respect themselves and other people.*

Over the years, scouting for both boys and girls in America has contributed to character and social development of young people. Recently, Frances Hasselbein and the National Girl Scout Organization have been commended for their management of community activities. The Girl Scouts have a membership of 2.5 million, about one in four American girls. Daisy Scouts now enroll 100,000 preschoolers, and new scouting programs include services for homeless girls. Girl Scout training involves weekly activities, selling cookies door-to-door and camping. Girl scouting supports public schools by providing training in personal and civic leadership through community service. It has 730,000 volunteers, including many young professional women, and 6,000 paid staff. Volunteer training for adults enhances parenting skills, develops community and professional leadership and supports public school activities.[34]

FINDING D: *African-American churches continue to play an important role in maintaining the cohesion of black society and the black family and in supporting public schools.*

Historically, the church has been the most important black cultural institution to protest against discrimination in public schools. Beginning in 1955, Martin Luther King, Jr. and a cadre of black clergy led the Montgomery bus boycott. Later, the Southern Christian Leadership Conference united diverse community-based civil rights groups. The landmark 1965 Federal Elementary and Secondary Education Act was the direct result of this civil rights protest. Many public school students and college students who protested later became national black political leaders. For many African Americans today, particularly the rural and urban poor, black churches still supply a significant network of family and educational support services. They also provide spiritual encouragement as alternatives to crime, drugs and urban gangs.[35]

FINDING E: *Community organizations help children by providing services that support education.*

In New York City, for example, United Way's CAPS program funds community-based organizations (CBOs) to provide educational support services. CBO staff members work with school staff to support learning by providing home visits, counseling, cultural and arts enrichment and learning opportunities through recreation. Bridging schools and their communities, more than 100 organizations have won contracts on a competitive basis that reach 25,000 youth. CAPS' budget, provided mainly by the board of education, includes corporate contributions.

FINDING F: *Athletic leagues with committed coaches can develop personal character, civic responsibility and academic achievement among disadvantaged youngsters in poverty-stricken urban public schools.*

In one of the nation's worst urban areas, Bob Shannon, an East St. Louis high school football coach, trains young men after school hours. They volunteer to become disciplined team members, responsible students and family members, classroom and community leaders. Some 60 percent of his players come from single-parent homes, and 80 percent receive public assistance. Despite such handicaps, Shannon has coached his high school teams to five state championships. This one teacher alone has saved hundreds of young black men from poverty, ignorance and wasted lives.[36]

MYTH #6: Employers are not major stakeholders in national public school reform.

American employers range from major corporations to small entrepreneurs, from public sector federal, state, and local governments to community and professional organizations and associations. While employers directly benefit from hiring graduates, most contribute very little to reforming public schools.

FINDING A: *Business requires a strong public education system to be profitable.*

Economic enterprise operates best within a system of law based on a viable civic culture where citizens—consumers, workers and employers alike—respect laws of property, contracts and taxation. The state licenses corporations to do business in the public interest. The state, not the market, legislates property rights, sets fair competition rules and enforces contracts. The state also operates the monetary system, encourages investment, provides basic transportation networks, maintains public order and educates the workers whose productivity yields profit. Both economic prosperity and a strong, healthy civic culture require an effective public education system.

FINDING B: *Workforce skills are the most significant factor in the productivity of any business.*

Public schools, which educate nine out of ten workers, provide the basic knowledge and skills that are the foundation for an organization's productivity and competitiveness. Workforce skills comprise 70 to 80 percent of manufacturing productivity and about 90 percent of service productivity. But new workers today have serious deficiencies in character and civic education, English, math, science, geography, history, foreign languages and information technologies. Remedial literacy training costs American employers approximately $30 billion annually. Added to this amount is the cost of accidents, security, shoddy workmanship, additional job training and interviewing excessive numbers of applicants to find the few qualified for entry-level jobs.

Employers who depend on workers with science backgrounds are recruiting from a shrinking pool of well-prepared students. This shortage is growing because of declining numbers of young qualified people, the retirement of experienced older workers and increased demand. Employers increasingly will depend on immigrants, as well as women and minorities. If the public schools continue to fail our students, the knowledge and skills of all American workers will continue to decline, the welfare costs will continue to rise and the tax burden on businesses and individuals will increase.

FINDING C: *A healthy American market requires prosperous and knowledgeable consumers as well as an educated, skilled workforce.*

Today's products are designed and targeted for better-educated and more-prosperous buyers. Because of this, market expansion requires consumers who can use and afford the products, technology and services.

Employers locate factories or service suppliers in communities having strong schools, industrious workers and public services such as libraries and transportation. States compete for large employers by having economic development strategies that include custom-fit employee training programs and tax incentives. To attract new businesses, the state of Iowa advertises that it has a better-educated, "smart" workforce.

Public school teachers and curriculum designers are most effective when informed by employers on worker skill needs, such as SCANS skills (Secretary's Commission on Achieving Necessary Skills), vocational skills and economic education. Where employees have been trained in personal and civic values, the costs of crime, theft, carelessness, mediocrity and sickness are reduced.

FINDING D: *Business charitable contributions are insignificant to the challenge of reforming the 83,500 public schools.*

Nationwide only about 6 percent of corporate giving for education goes to public elementary and secondary education.

The remainder goes to private schools, colleges and universities. After the cost of overhead and public relations, this contribution amounts to *about $6 per public school student per year. By contrast, the federal government alone puts over $600 million or $600 per student annually into New York City public schools.* Corporate grants made directly to schools often are given for public relations value or in the context of gift-matching. These grants seldom are targeted strategically, monitored or evaluated. Most corporate executives do not understand the cultures of public schools nor do they understand how to leverage the huge government investments in public education. They largely ignore state and federal education committee legislators, who spend billions of corporate and personal tax dollars and set public policy in education that affects long-term corporate survival. They rarely support public-policy education research with significant contributions, yet public policy leadership is the corporate world's most effective contribution to school reform.

Some corporations are increasing their funding for school reform organizations. The Business Roundtable, The National Alliance of Business, The Conference Board and the Committee for Economic Development are leading national business associations whose executives are struggling with public education reform.

MYTH #7: The federal government has little responsibility for American public school education.

FINDING A: *The federal government has clear constitutional and legislative authority in public education.*

The 10th Amendment to the Constitution reserves powers not delegated to the federal government for the states *and the people.* Through their representatives, the American people have delegated the primary responsibility for financing and governing public schools to the states and their local education agencies. Historically, the federal government has provided educational leadership by launching grammar schools with the Northwest Ordinance of 1787, starting the land-grant colleges and universities with the Morrill Act of

1862. In this century, it initiated programs in vocational education, special education, international education and early-childhood education. In addition, the president and congressional leaders have designated the federal government as a partner in providing educational opportunity, conducting educational research and assessment, funding education for the disadvantaged and improving educational competitiveness for all Americans. The Supreme Court has consistently upheld the federal authority in these areas.

Almost a decade after Congress established the cabinet-level Department of Education, it passed the Omnibus Trade and Competitiveness Act of 1988. This landmark legislation linked federal education policy to promoting productivity and national competitiveness in our global economy. The act set federal policy to enhance elementary and secondary education, to assist functionally illiterate youth and adults who are out of school, and to help schools modernize laboratory and technical equipment and expand instruction in mathematics, sciences and foreign languages.

America 2000, President Bush's 1990 education initiative, legitimated an expanded federal education role by taking even greater responsibility for the quality of local elementary and secondary education:

"While the federal government's role in education is and should remain limited, the administration is committed to providing R&D, assessment and information, assuring equal opportunity and ... leading the nationwide effort to achieve the six education goals. When goals are set and strategies for achieving them are adopted, we must establish clear measures of performance and then issue annual report cards on the progress of students, schools, the states, and the federal government."[37]

Over the past decade, a political stalemate has developed over education policy between the Democratic Congress and Republican White House. The stalemate has paralyzed the federal government as a significant force in helping to transform our deteriorating public education system.

Today, dynamic federal leadership is required to carry

out the federal role in education as mandated by the Constitution and Congress:[38]

- assuring equal opportunity by enforcing laws pertaining to civil rights
- defining national goals, standards, assessments
- disseminating information on the condition of American education
- providing additional resources to increase all students' achievement of these standards
- investing in effective educational research and demonstration models of responsible learning cultures
- assessing federal program impact on student achievement at the school-site level
- disseminating quality models of education improvement to all students, parents, workers, schools, postsecondary institutions, communities, corporations, states and federal agencies

In the 1980s, as total government revenues and the national income grew, federal funds for elementary and secondary education actually declined, as adjusted for inflation. The federal government tries to ensure that disadvantaged children and adults who receive federal aid are "eligible" for services. Few administrators of federal education and training program funds are accountable to Congress for evaluation of programmatic impact on participants. Even more important, federal resources are not being leveraged for improved learning. A 1992 Gallup Poll indicated low public regard for presidential and congressional leadership in improving public schools. Respondents' rating of the President were 15 percent A or B and 46 percent D or F, while the Congress received 7 percent A or B and 52 percent D or F.[39]

FINDING B: *The best-kept secret today is that the federal government has the largest education and training budget in the world!*

Federal resources address the nation's most difficult education problems and affect most students and educational institutions. According to the National Center for Educational Statistics, the federal government supports over 140 separate education programs in 25 department, agencies and institutions. Programs include compensatory education, postsecondary education, educational research and improvement, worker preparation and training, and the Department of Agriculture's school breakfast, lunch and milk programs. The largest programs are administered by the Department of Education, which accounts for about 50 percent of all federal education and research program support.

In 1992, over $48 billion will be spent on federal education and training programs in America's schools and colleges. This is in addition to $19.5 billion in tax credits, $14 billion in funds generated from other sources (largely for guaranteed student loans) and $14.6 billion in research contracts to colleges and universities, reaching a total impact of $96 billion. This is the equivalent of 23 percent of the $405 billion budgeted for all public and private educational institutions in the United States.

FINDING C: *According to the U.S. Department of Education, the federal government's contribution to the cost of public elementary and secondary education actually is $22.5 billion or 10 percent not the widely reported 6.2 percent.*

Of the $225 billion spent on public K–12 education in America, $22.5 billion is federal money. This amount does not include $2 billion funding for Head Start, which remains the only publicly-funded early-childhood program in many of the states. Nor does it include either the $5.2 billion Department of Agriculture lunch and breakfast programs or the $385 million budget for TRIO programs, which mainly prepare disadvantaged high school students for college. Also it does not include the Federal tax deduction for local property taxes, which are largely dedicated to the public schools. Federal funding included here is for compensatory education, math, science, vocational, bilingual and special education, as well as for the two school systems for which the federal government has 100 percent of the responsibility: Bureau of Indian Affairs Schools and the Department of Defense Dependents Schools, which is the nation's ninth largest school district. Federal support varies from 4 to 80 percent, constituting a greater-than-average share of total funding in the largest cities, poorest states and overseas territories. Beyond direct funding to public schools, the federal government supports 80 percent of the nation's educational research and provides student financial aid to half of all college students preparing to teach in the public schools.

FINDING D: *The federal government's most effective youth-at-risk training program is Job Corps.*

Job Corps is a 28-year-old solution for some of the major problems faced today by impoverished and at-risk youths. The average youth helped at Job Corps is 18 years old, has a family income of $5,803 per year, reads below the eighth grade level, is a high school dropout and has never worked full time. Job Corps has bipartisan support in Congress and has assisted over 1.5 million young people who might otherwise have ended up costing the taxpayer thousands of dollars in legal, court and jail costs (up to $30,000 annually) or welfare. The Job Corps curriculum includes educational and vocational training, job search and placement services, medical and dental care and drug abuse treatment. Job Corps targets these disadvantaged 16- to 21-year-olds and, in a disciplined, residential setting, sets out to turn these youths into self-sufficient, educated and productive members of society for an average cost to the taxpayers of $12,000 per trainee.

In summary, the federal government is the only institution that regulates both public and private sectors and represents the national interest. With dynamic leadership the federal government could become the most significant player in the new American Knowledge Revolution.[40]

MYTH #8: Americans cannot afford to invest more money in public school reform.

All American taxpayers support public schools by paying individual federal, state and local income, corporate, property or sales taxes. Voters and elected public officials decide the spending priorities. If properly managed and adequately financed, public school investments can offer the greatest economic return for all Americans.

FINDING A: *Each individual's standard of living is affected by his/her own and other Americans' skills and productivity.*

During the 1970s and 1980s, achievement scores of high school graduates declined and U.S. productivity growth slowed by three-fifths, from 2.9 percent to 1.2 percent. Because the higher productivity of the 1950s and 1960s was not maintained, each American lost a total of $28,000 in his/her standard of living in the next two decades. As a result of slower growth in skills, productivity and income, Americans are compensating by working 9 percent more hours, or an extra month per year.

Although most skilled workers experienced real wage increases, over 13 million less-skilled workers experienced real wage decreases.[41] Across the 1980s, for example, the purchasing power of families in the bottom tenth of the income scale dropped by nearly 15 percent, approximately $2,850. By contrast, the purchasing power of those in the top tenth rose nearly 17 percent, almost $90,000.[42]

Knowledge gained in the public schools leads to greater worker skills. The most significant factor in productivity today is worker skills, which contribute 65 percent to 80 percent in manufacturing and up to 90 percent in knowledge-intensive service industries. The key to increasing individual productivity and standard of living, therefore, is investment in human resources. Human resource development also attracts investments in R&D, high-tech equipment and structures. Our nation can only be competitive tomorrow if we wisely invest scarce resources today.[43]

FINDING B: *Present expenditures for public elementary and secondary education are inadequate to match the student achievements of our competitors.*

U.S. public schools are graduating students whose achievement scores are consistently below those of international competitors. Although 90 percent of all American workers are products of K–12 public schooling, the U.S. spends only 3.6 percent of its Gross Domestic Product (GDP), or about $225 billion in 1993 on public schooling ($5,665 per student each year). Other modern nations spend more; Sweden spends 7 percent.[44]

An adequate investment strategy for reforming our primary and secondary education, however, will require more than just matching the expenditures of other countries. The objective is to achieve comparable performance by students so that we are individually and nationally competitive. Due to years of neglect, a more diverse population and growing numbers of disadvantaged children, a greater investment will be required to catch up with the performance of students in competitor nations.

FINDING C: *Without major reform, simply investing more money in an ineffective public school system will not make America competitive.*

The present annual expenditures of $225 billion for public schools represents a significant and imperative reform opportunity. If the productivity of school administrators and teachers is increased by only 3.2 percent each year, as measured by increased student achievement, the performance of public schools could be increased 34 percent in 10 years without additional investments beyond today's costs. In any case, we must close the achievement gap within 10 years. It should be understood that the gains needed cannot be achieved without investment in reform.

FINDING D: *Federal funding reflects national priorities.*

Taxpayers have paid $47 billion in research for the Strategic Defense Initiative (SDI) and will pay $200 billion over a five-year period for the cost of the savings and loan bailout. American citizens have supported federal expenditures they believed were necessary. They have financed world wars, European and Asian recovery after World War II and missions to the moon. While supporting international and national defense commitments, they funded the mammoth G.I. Bill which provide educational opportunities for 20 million veterans. *There is no other public investment that can match education for significantly improving the standard of living of all Americans!*

LEADERSHIP: Responsible Learning Cultures

Economic competitiveness requires workers and managers whose values, knowledge and skills lead to high productivity. Investment in educational reform will be wasted unless we, as change agents, create responsible learning cultures. Success in our global knowledge economy requires cultural adaptations of the magnitude comparable to those associated with the Reformation, the Renaissance and the Industrial Revolution. Education and leadership are the means to cultural transformations and economic growth. These cultural transformations will involve our families, schools, workplaces and governments.

Culture is a "mental map" of stable ideas—shared values, attitudes and strategies—that has the power to shape society and its individuals. Culture helps people deal with their daily lives by indicating what is important and providing guidelines to follow. Individual patterns or strategies of behavior are organized around dominant cultural values. For example, raising children is handled within the family, while knowledge and skills are acquired largely through the education system. A group or society advances and prospers when its culture incorporates a particular cluster of "primary" values—respect for family, community, work, entrepreneurship, education, austerity and excellence. Without this cluster of values, cultures tend to resist change and the society declines.[45]

Cultural patterns are formed or changed when individuals in a group or society confront similar problems and devise solutions. If a solution works well, it may become a "cultural response" and be passed on to new members. Each person belongs to several groups that compete for attention and commitment. Individuals alter their cultural understandings as they try the cultural responses of their different group memberships and experience the consequences. The cultural messages are transmitted formally and informally through rules and codes, ideologies and folk beliefs, stories and scripts, jargon and jokes, music and rap, rituals and ceremonies. Each group to which a person belongs competes for attention and commitment.

Culture is carried by the individual. Only individuals have minds in which to store interpretations and cultural responses to challenges. Only individuals can accept or reject these responses, but groups or networks of support are necessary to sustain culture. When outside challenges overwhelm the traditional cultural response, the group begins to disintegrate and individuals begin to malfunction. Leaders emerge offering new strategies which, if accepted by members of the group, become a new cultural response.

The Leadership Factor

The leadership commitment and skills of each individual are crucial to developing responsible learning cultures. Leaders reconcile the culture's values and responses to changing environmental needs.[46] They introduce policies and rules—potential cultural strategies—that can be added, discarded or reprioritized. If they *communicate* their *vision* effectively, others are motivated to carry out the innovations. These changes gradually may be embedded in the culture.

Parents, educators, public officials, businesses and community leaders can develop leadership skills to create responsible cultures. Such cultures would value, as a top priority, individual development through lifelong education and training. Such responsible learning cultures would structure time and energy to create an environment for children and adults to make choices, to experience consequences and to continue learning.

Leadership skills necessary to introduce and bring about this cultural change include:

- *assessing* strengths and weaknesses of individuals and the group

- *creating a clear vision* with three or four initial priorities, using inputs from others in the group or organization
- *communicating* this vision persuasively to others
- *identifying* real problems and brainstorming possible solutions
- *designing written strategies*, policies and operational guidelines
- *implementing action plans* with clear goals
- *assessing and sharing* regularly the progress toward agreed-upon goals with all participants

Our global economic challenges put at risk our economic prosperity, quality of life and political stability. *To become competitive again, each American must participate in transforming our learning culture at all levels.* We must revitalize the values and traditions of our national civic culture and develop strategies to realign them with our rapidly changing economy. *Courageous leaders in every institution of American society must begin rebuilding our larger community culture by declaring war against ignorance and organizing responsible learning cultures in every organization to which we belong.* Our individual, group and national actions will fail without individuals forming knowledge support networks and taking dramatic action to bring about this critical cultural change—the Knowledge Revolution.

AN ACTION PLAN FOR ALL AMERICANS: Building Responsible Learning Cultures

To succeed in making all Americans educationally competitive, we must empower public schools. We must forge linkages between schools and support groups such as families, higher educators, community organizations, businesses, government and media. Parents are the most important stakeholders in creating these linkages for their children. But to make our public schools world-class, responsible learning cultures for the nation's children, all of us must participate in the war against ignorance.[47] Only through responsible action and personal sacrifice of time, energy and money can we, the American people, carry out the Knowledge Revolution for our children's and the nation's future.

Learning Improvement Contract

The strategy for establishing effective linkages among essential partners to improve learning is to develop agreed-upon action plans. Learning Improvement Contracts (LICs) can be developed between public schools and parents, employers, higher educators, media and community leaders. They are not legally binding but are moral commitments agreed upon by all parties. (For an example, see Appendices.)[48]

A LIC is an inexpensive, non-bureaucratic leadership tool. It defines purposes and provides guidelines, and thereby motivates action. The process of creating a LIC has several benefits for each partner: (1) requires assessment of needs and defines expectations; (2) identifies three or four ways a partner can contribute to improving the child's learning; (3) designs a written action plan outlining specific steps that will be taken to achieve the objectives; (4) reserves the hours required weekly/monthly to carry out the personal or institutional plan;

and (5) assesses each month the progress made toward meeting the objectives.

The following are examples of "what works"—individual and organizational actions that researchers and other Knowledge Revolutionaries have found to be successful. Review the recommendations for creating responsible learning cultures that support individual ongoing education. Help start the Knowledge Revolution now!

EMPOWERING THE FAMILY. Family Actions and LICs Could Include:

1. **Parents' Leadership Commitment.** Parents should commit to transform or create a responsible learning culture in their family by:
   - preparing their children to enter school ready to learn
   - collaborating with their children, extended family, school officials and community leaders
   - working to elect and supporting qualified community leaders as school board members
2. **Parent Training.** Parents should prepare to nurture and train their child for school by:
   - completing parent-as-educator workshops
   - teaching appropriate character and citizenship values and behavior
   - teaching knowledge and skills necessary for becoming responsible family members, students, workers, consumers and community members
   - teaching "foundation skills"—character development, personal care, nutrition and exercise, interpersonal communication, household maintenance, financial resource management
   - supporting their child's school goals and activities, limiting television and part-time employment, monitoring homework, reading aloud, and providing space, time and other study resources

3. **Evaluation and Accountability.** Parents should collaborate with teachers and principals on what their child is expected to achieve during the year by:
   - assessing needs of health, knowledge and skills, compared with state, national and world-class standards
   - reviewing before-after achievement scores with their child and teachers at the close of each semester and participating in updating the student's LIC for the next semester
   - providing a written "report card" evaluation to the school principal and school board on the contributions of teachers and counselors in improving their child's knowledge at the end of each school year

For additional information on how to design a family Learning Improvement Contract (LIC), call the Knowledge Network at 1-800-736-4877 and refer to message #4001.

EMPOWERING THE PUBLIC SCHOOL. Public School Actions and LICs Could Include:

1. **Educator's Leadership Commitment.** School board members, superintendents, principals and teachers should commit to collaborate with parents and community representatives in creating a responsible school learning culture with school-site-based budgeting and performance management.
2. **Educator Training.** For professional contract renewal, educators should facilitate student acquisition of knowledge by obtaining training and demonstrating mastery in:
   - knowing their subject matter
   - teaching with interactive group skills
   - using learning technologies, computers, distance learning, telecommunication networks and voice mail to communicate with parents on a daily or other regular basis
   - creating safe, cohesive, supportive learning environments

- assessing student performance

3. **Character and Citizenship Education.** Principals should appoint a task force of parents, students and teachers to develop an effective program for character and citizenship education to be implemented and evaluated by the close of each school year.
4. **Curriculum and Standards.** Principals should appoint teachers to adapt curriculum and learning activities so that, prior to beginning their senior year, students demonstrate mastery of:
    - "foundation skills"—character development, personal management, reading, writing, arithmetic and communication
    - "central skills"—planning, information processing, technology usage, interpersonal relations and citizenship, including participation in public service projects
    - world-class standards in English, mathematics, science, social studies, foreign language, computer sciences, arts and humanities
    - health knowledge and physical education training
    - nonviolent expression of anger by learning to negotiate differences
5. **Teachers.** Teachers should, with parental involvement, develop effective in-class teaching models that demonstrate:
    - dynamic, experiential learning activities with high expectations for each student
    - accelerated instruction that actively engages students' interests and develops analytic and problem-solving skills
    - creative use of community resources
    - closing the individual student achievement gaps as identified in each student's LIC by Fall enrollment for advancement to the next grade level
6. **Students.** Students should:
    - complete regular and challenging homework

- be able to accelerate learning and bypass standard courses by demonstrating mastery of subject matter and receiving course credit
- participate in before- and after-school, Saturday, and summer educational activities when they are not meeting world-class academic standards

7. **Coalition Building.** Principals and teachers should work with parents to:
   - support school goals and activities
   - limit television and part-time employment, except for apprenticeship programs
   - monitor homework and reading assignments
   - provide space, time and necessary resources to complete homework assignments
   - provide multiple models of participation for parents with different skill levels—including group process and interpersonal skills, language and literature training—so that parents can respond to the school's outreach on behalf of their child
   - provide orientation for parents and prospective kindergartners prior to their entering the public school system
   - provide facilities for before- and after-school multi-service use: public health, recreation, welfare, job counseling, adult and arts education, and libraries
8. **Evaluation and Accountability.** Principals and teachers should:
   - conduct a needs assessment of student knowledge and skills as a basis for constructing their LIC with students and parents
   - evaluate achievement of management and learning objectives defined in their annual professional performance review
   - review before-after achievement scores with students and their parents at the close of each semester
   - evaluate participation of parents in carrying out their

LIC responsibilities to improve their children's achievement

- provide comparative information on classroom-, school-, and district-level performance to local media by the close of each school year
- receive a substantial merit increase in pay for each student in their classes/school who achieves or makes significant gains toward world-class performance as defined in the individual student LIC

For additional information on how to design public school Learning Improvement Contracts (LICs), call the Knowledge Network at 1-800-736-4877 and refer to message #4002.

EMPOWERING HIGHER EDUCATION. Higher Education Actions and LICs Could Include:

1. **Higher Educators' Leadership Commitment.** College and university presidents should:
    - conduct an in-depth strategic review of all programs that could directly impact public schools
    - significantly improve their institution's contribution to two or more local public schools within 12 months

2. **Teacher Training.** Faculty should prepare elementary and secondary teachers to demonstrate mastery in:
    - teaching to world-class standards
    - character and citizenship education and multicultural intergroup relations
    - teaching techniques that create safe, cohesive, supportive environments for interactive group experiences that also facilitate individual learning
    - using learning technologies, computers, telecommunication networks and voice mail
    - directing experiential learning that helps students synthesize theory and practice
    - participating on an effective teaching team in school-site management
    - assessing student performance

3. **Curriculum and Standards.** Teacher educators should:
   - incorporate world-class standards in teaching
   - ensure that all graduating teachers meet world-class standards within three years
4. **Research, Dissemination and Assessment.** Educators should:
   - disseminate their publicly sponsored education research to public and private schools through an expanded Department of Education diffusion network
   - develop assessment instruments for world-class standards
5. **Coalition Building.** College and university officials should:
   - create a partnership with several local schools
   - conduct a needs assessment to identify what the higher education institution can contribute to the local school
   - set aside a portion of their annual budgets for faculty and students to invest in public school research, training and consulting activities
   - provide incentives for their students to participate in community partnerships that support public school reform
   - collaborate, with federal support, to provide technical assistance from strong teacher education programs to those institutions identified by regional accreditation agencies as needing help to achieve world-class standards
6. **Evaluation and Accountability.** College and university officials should:
   - evaluate their contribution to building stronger elementary and secondary schools and to improving student achievement as defined by their LIC
   - publish an annual report of their accomplishments for the board of trustees, alumni and media

EMPOWERING COMMUNITY ORGANIZATIONS. Community Organization Actions and LICs Could Include:

1. **Community Leadership Commitment.** Community leaders should:
    - visit neighborhood public schools and explore with the principals ways in which their organization's mission, activities and membership could support public and private school activities
    - develop a five-year strategic management plan for their organizations to support schools with targets, timetables, budgets, roles and accountability measures for presentation to their board of directors
    - spend at least one day per month coordinating joint public school activities with educators and other community leaders
2. **Character, Citizenship and Academic Training.** Community leaders should:
    - organize parent-educator training workshops for all adult volunteers and professional staff members
    - focus outreach parent-training workshops for disadvantaged single mothers
    - revise and strengthen character education and citizenship training of all association members
3. **Leadership Development.** Since United Way funds many community organizations, its executives should:
    - require public school reform training for all executives of organizations receiving funding
    - provide budget incentives for community organizations whose members and staff participate in public school reform
4. **Coalition Building.** Community leaders should:
    - identify and form neighborhood public school partnerships with targeted objectives and successful evaluation indicators for both parties in a written community

association LIC signed by top school board officials and community association leaders

- coordinate education participation with other community leaders to avoid duplication of efforts
- recruit student and adult volunteers to tutor and organize extracurricular activities as needed in selected public schools

5. **Evaluation and Accountability.** Community leaders should:
   - assist the school boards in publishing student achievement scores by school through local media
   - evaluate their association's contributions to public school reform during the past year as defined by their community association's Learning Improvement Contract

For additional information on how to design a Learning Improvement Contract (LIC), call the Knowledge Network at 1-800-736-4877 and refer to message #4004.

EMPOWERING EMPLOYERS. Employer Actions and LICs Could Include:

1. **Business Executives Leadership Commitment.** Employers should:
   - request a comprehensive assessment of educational philanthropic grants and employee time contributions to reforming public elementary and secondary schools during the previous year
   - develop a five-year plan by defining management and accounting procedures and roles and by targeting corporate contributions
   - collaborate with a local school or school system to develop a LIC
   - invest one day per month or more of revenue time in directing corporate resources to assist community and national public school reform
   - become acting principal or teacher for a day

- recognize corporate employees who contribute to improving public schools

2. **Worker and Management Training.** Employers should direct corporate training personnel to:
    - make available parent-educator training workshops to all employees for developing their own family LICs
    - provide high school students with internships, career and vocational training opportunities
    - provide teachers with summer jobs to supplement their income and broaden their experience
    - recruit all qualified high school graduates by eliminating racial, ethnic, gender and disabled discrimination from corporate workplaces
    - request high school transcripts as a condition of employment and publicize this practice
    - invite local school administrators to participate without charge in management training programs
    - provide corporate executives and managers with experience in public school cultures
3. **Coalition Building.** Employers should:
    - work with local superintendents and principals to develop creative school/corporate partnerships using targeted corporate resources and volunteer employees and retirees as teachers, teacher aides and tutors
    - participate in systemic education reform at the state level by chambers of commerce and the Business Roundtable's Nine Point Reform Agenda; and at the urban school-district level, such as Los Angeles' LEARN community alliance
    - participate in national and federal education policy reform through the National Alliance of Business
    - testify before local school boards, governors and state legislatures on the need for world-class teacher education standards, SCANS skills (Secretary's Commission on Achieving Necessary Skills) and changing job-skill requirements

- testify before congressional education committees on the need for world-class standards in such programs as Head Start, Chapter 1, vocational education, science education, arts and humanities, and international education for future workers in the global knowledge economy
- fund promising public policy research leading to effective educational reform and investment

4. **Evaluation and Accountability.** Employers should:
    - distinguish between accounts for valid public relations education activities and corporate contributions to systemic public school reform
    - conduct for the board of directors a policy evaluation study on the effectiveness of corporate employee participation, executive leadership, education grants and taxes in improving public education over the past five years
    - evaluate their contributions to public school reform during the past year as defined by their corporation's LIC and other reform efforts

For additional information on how to design an employer Learning Improvement Contract (LIC), call the Knowledge Network at 1-800-736-4877 and refer to message #4005.

EMPOWERING MASS MEDIA. Media Actions and LICs Could Include:

1 **Media Leadership Commitment.** Media executives should:
- appoint a top executive to manage a new "education services" division and develop special media and community recognition programs
- request a comprehensive assessment of reporting coverage and quality of primary and secondary education stories and air time exposure for the previous year
- develop a viable one-year plan to improve public schools by committing organization leadership and

resources to improving coverage of positive reform activities in proportion to the potential audience of educators, parents, workers and interested citizens

- commit a portion of institutional program budgets to specials about successful public school reforms
- invest one day per month or more of executive time to assist in community and national public school reform
- design and implement an incentive system and recognition program for employees who contribute to improving public schools

2. **Worker and Management Training.** Media executives should:
   - provide employees with parent-educator training workshops
   - work with board members, superintendents, principals, and outstanding teachers to conduct employee workshops at local public schools

3. **Coalition Building.** Media executives should:
   - collaborate with local superintendents to develop creative media/school partnerships using volunteer employees and retirees as teachers, teacher aides and tutors and report their experiences
   - offer school officials and public information officers the opportunity to receive advanced training in media/school relations
   - explore joint ventures to promote wider coverage on the value of competitive knowledge to all Americans with other media executives
   - develop a community "learning partners" program to train parents on ways to use media to improve a child's literacy
   - recognize outstanding contributions by parents, students, teachers, administrators and school board members
   - report student performance information at the classroom, school, district and state level as compared to world-class standards

EMPOWERING FEDERAL GOVERNMENT CONTRIBUTIONS TO PUBLIC SCHOOLS—THE KNOWLEDGE REVOLUTION ACT OF 1993

1. **The President should:**
    - report to the nation semiannually on the progress of national public education reform as it relates to improving global competitiveness
    - submit annual federal budgets that demonstrate how each major expenditure advances the national learning priorities and improves the skills and performance of students, families and workers
    - direct each executive agency to prepare strategic blueprints showing how each program to be funded will advance the new overall federal education and training mission of reforming American public schools

2. **Congress and the President should enact the "Knowledge Revolution Act" of 1993.** The act should mobilize parents and public, private and community leaders to transform the nation's schools into responsible learning cultures. Proposed provisions:

    A. **Federal Education and Training Resource Management.** The Act should authorize the appropriation of **high-performance incentive funds** that implement LICs and improve student performance by:
    - enabling school district officials to design LICs making them eligible for new federal high-performance funds
    - retraining federal, state and local administrators in the use of federal resources, not as entitlements, but as taxpayer investments for improving the performance of public school students
    - retraining the nation's public and private school administrators and teachers in dynamic, participative management and high-technology methods

    B. **Educational Research and Dissemination.** Since the U.S. Department of Education funds over 80 percent of America's education research, the Act should direct the Secretary to:

- establish a distinguished panel of principals, superintendents and teachers to advise the Secretary on educational research projects to be funded with federal taxes
- disseminate "best educational practices" that improve public and private schooling
- disseminate the latest technology and new teaching approaches
- disseminate knowledge about practices that improve literacy for disadvantaged students, parents, workers and all adults

C. **Curriculum and Standards.** The Act should enable the Secretary of Education to:

- coordinate public and private efforts to establish national goals, academic standards and student assessment in physical, biological, and social science education, humanities and arts education and physical education
- fund colleges and universities to provide technical assistance in revising curriculum and retraining teachers and administrators with competitive knowledge and skills
- provide funds to strong schools of education to assist other institutions in achieving world-class standards in teacher preparation
- fund implementation of SCANS—planning information, technology, interpersonal and systems skills development and assessment for all 15- to 16-year-olds

D. **Disadvantaged and Other Students.** The Act should:

- target Chapter 1 funds for new "public enterprise centers" that show how disadvantaged students can accelerate their learning and performance

- support education and training programs that demonstrate new interactive group learning and technology use
- introduce differential pay, up to 25 percent, to "supplement" the salaries of local teachers—in such federal programs as Head Start, Chapter 1, special education, bilingual education, science education and skill-shortage fields—who demonstrate that their students made significant improvement toward meeting world-class standards

E. **Workforce Preparation, At-Risk Youth.** The Act should:

- provide for a national youth apprenticeship program, linking it to the secondary school curriculum
- in accordance with the proposed "50/50 plan," double the size of Job Corps by the year 2000, serving one in four at-risk youths, as opposed to the one in seven eligible young people currently helped
- establish a separate Model Job Corps Alternative Sentencing Option (AS0) for youths who have entered the Criminal Justice System, saving the taxpayer prison, maintenance and court costs and reducing recidivism rates
- re-open closed military bases to serve as training centers for youths

F. **Coalition Building.** The Act should:

- require the Secretary of Education to coordinate all federal education activities under the Federal Interagency Committee on Education (FICE)
- require the Secretary of Education to have all schools receiving federal aid organize parent/teacher school councils to advise principals on spending federal funds and accounting for its impact

- enable the Secretaries of Education and Labor to sponsor reform conferences that include such national groups as the National Board for Professional Teaching Standards, the National Goals Commission, the National Alliance of Business, the Conference Board, the Business Roundtable, the American Society for Training and Development, the Education Commission of the States, the National School Boards Association, the American Association of School Administrators, the National Education Association and the American Federation of Teachers
- establish a National Advisory Council on Education and Training Excellence, composed of leaders in education, business, community and government to advise the Secretary of Education quarterly on vocational education for career preparation

G. **Evaluation and Accountability.** The Act should direct the President to:

- have cabinet officers evaluate all federal education and training programs on their success in helping educators and parents improve student, parent and public school performance
- have the Secretary of Education use NAEP for regularly assessing the performance of American students in relation to the world-class standards achieved by other countries
- have the Secretary of Education require local educational or training organizations that receive federal high-performance funds report results of student testing by classroom and school to all major stakeholders—parents, students, community, state and federal taxpayers—through appropriate media sources
- forgive federal student loans for those who teach in public schools for at least five years

WHAT WILL IT COST THE NATION TO BECOME COMPETITIVE AGAIN?

Americans must gain a greater return on their educational investment by implementing a strategy of reform that focuses on LICs at every level of schooling. Without successful high-performance investment and LICs to reform and empower public schools, no amount of additional investment will make public schools competitive. *Public officials should only allocate high-performance funding to school districts that agree to demonstrate significant student improvement.* Educational reform has failed when not requiring change and accountability for both current and additional spending to raise student performance.

1. **Federal, state and local governments should increase investments for all American students to improve their performance by:**
    - **high-performance investment.** Over 10 years, governments should phase in an allocation of 1 percent more of our national income (GDP) as high-performance investments for public elementary and secondary education. Starting with 1993, all levels of government combined should provide at least $6.3 billion more each year, rising to at least $63 billion in the 10th year, and equalling at least $315 billion during 10 years. This increase would affect only a small 0.3 percent of the governments' expenditures each year. It would amount to about $150 more per student in the 1st year, rising to at least $1,500 by the 10th year, and totalling at least $7,500 during the 10 years (in 1993 dollars).
    - **driving high-performance investment.** The governments should provide high-performance investments above 1993 levels only if a feasible LIC is developed with parents and students, and then submitted by teachers and administrators in each district to state education agencies and elected officials. The LIC must demonstrate commitment and certifiable progress of 3.2 percent or more in student

achievement each year. This is based on the productivity growth required from all working Americans to catch up with competitors. In addition, educators must show that gains made will close the knowledge gap within 10 years. At this rate, U.S. student achievement should match that of major competitors like France, Germany and Japan within 10 years. The additional spending, particularly the federal share, should give priority to improving the performance of the educationally disadvantaged, who represent approximately one out of every four students. They should receive about $1,800 per student by the 10th year or $9,000 over the 10 year period. Significant funds, $1,400 per student by the 10th year or $7,000 during the 10 years, should be spent on improving the performance of the other 75 percent of American students. Competitiveness requires all students to perform to their full capabilities.

- **reform dividends.** Additional high performance investment must require at least 3.2 percent greater student performance from current appropriated and tax expenditures each year. The "reform dividend" would be equivalent to $7.2 billion or $170 per student in the 1st year, $83 billion or $2,000 per student in the 10th year. Cumulatively, this would be $385 billion or $9,500 per student during the 10 years. In time, this huge reform dividend could be used to reduce the annual new educational investments.

Accordingly, the percentage of GDP committed to the public schools could decline. The share of GDP now being invested in public elementary and secondary education is about 3.6 percent, according to U.S. Department of Education statistics. The new annual $6.3 billion investment each year would have the effect of increasing the percentage of GDP toward 4.6 within 10 years. Thereafter, the reform dividend would make it possible to reduce this percentage of GDP to around 4.1 percent, still providing enough investment for the more disadvantaged student populations.

The potential gains from reform dividends dramatize the enormous benefit of the Knowledge Revolution to all Americans. These gains represent the value added from restructuring schooling and improving content, teaching and assessment of learning.

2. **The federal government should provide for educationally disadvantaged students each year through high school graduation by:**
   - **high-performance investment.** In 1991, the federal government appropriated about $22.5 billion, or 10 percent of the total cost for public schools. It also allowed modest tax expenditures—such as personal income tax deductions of property taxes—which support public schools. The recommendations outlined require the federal government to increase its public school support by $3.8 billion or nearly $100 per student in the 1st year. The additional support would grow to $38 billion or $900 per student by the 10th year, and $190 billion or $4,500 per student during 10 years. The federal government would provide 60 percent of new investment and increase its overall support from more than 10 to 22 percent. Yet the federal share would only affect 2.5 percent of the federal budget annually.
   - **reform dividends.** The federal government's direct responsibility for improving the results of its spending and tax provisions are modest, about $0.8 billion in the 1st year, $9 billion in the 10th year, and $45 billion or about $1,100 per student during 10 years. The federal government, however, has the opportunity to encourage state and local governments to meet their reform requirements, particularly for disadvantaged students.
3. **State and local governments should provide new:**
   - **high-performance investment.** In 1991, state and local governments spent approximately $202.5 billion to support the public schools, representing 90 percent of total costs. The recommendations outlined require

state and local governments to increase their public school expenditures by $2.5 billion in the 1st year or $25 billion by the 10th year. Over the decade, this would amount to $125 billion or $3,000 per student. This would allow state and local governments to invest only 40 percent of the new money and lower their share of both current and new spending from about 90 percent to 78 percent. It would only affect 2.7 percent of state and local expenditures in any year.

- **reform dividends**. Their portion (nearly 90 percent) of the reform dividend should be equivalent to $6.4 billion in the 1st year, rising to $75 billion by the 10th year. Over the 10 years, this would be $370 billion or $8,800 per student. State and local governments should place less reliance on property taxes as a source of education funds because of the inherent deficiencies and distortions. The modestly increasing federal role should partially compensate for these weaknesses.

4. **Private school actions:**
    - School officials should seek additional private resources for innovative programs and for summer, weekend and tutorial services which could assist public and private students. These activities could attract additional revenue of $2 billion each year and $20 billion by the 10th year, a total of $100 billion over the 10 year period.
    - Supporters of private schools should insist on at least a 3.2 percent annual improvement in student performance. They should do their share in closing the national knowledge gap within 10 years. This reform dividend would be equivalent to at least $0.8 billion in the 1st year, $9 billion by the 10th year—a total of $43 billion and $9,500 per student over the 10 years.

Elementary and secondary school investments and reform dividends must be combined with those proposed for preschool, postsecondary education and worker retraining. In these areas, there should be about three times more new-dollar investments and two times more reform dividends than is outlined for elementary and secondary education. While federal, state and local governments are the primary sources for these gains in elementary and secondary schools, the private sector plays the major role in preschool and worker training. These investments and reforms, along with complementary R&D and physical capital investments, will enable the U.S. to increase income growth (GDP) by one percentage point, from 2.2 to 3.2 percent within 10 years. This major improvement in individual and national productivity will make America competitive again.

THE THIRD AMERICAN REVOLUTION: Competitive Knowledge for All Americans

In early December 1774, following the battles at Lexington and Bunker Hill, John Adams, Benjamin Rush, Benjamin Franklin and George Washington met to review the rising tensions with England. Franklin introduced the others to an Englishman, Thomas Paine, who stunned his hosts by speaking forcefully for American independence. Washington requested that Paine publish his startling views. On January 10, 1776, *Common Sense*, the first policy statement advocating an American revolution, was published. Within the first year, the 47-page political tract sold 150,000 copies.[49] Six months later, the Declaration of Independence was drafted by Thomas Jefferson and signed by 55 other American patriots who pledged to each other their lives, fortunes and sacred honor. During the Revolutionary War, Paine captured the meaning of these events, "These are the times that try men's souls. The summer soldier and the sunshine patriot will, in this crisis, shrink from the service of his country; but he that stands it NOW, deserves the love and thanks of man and woman."

In 1788, another national advocacy document helped save the Constitution of this newly independent nation. *The Federalist Papers* by Alexander Hamilton, James Madison and John Jay were published as newspaper editorials in New York City. They were circulated in Virginia and New York—two states crucial for ratification. Virginia delegates ratified the Constitution by only 10 votes (89 to 79); in New York, ratification carried by only three (30 to 27).[50] It would take another 200 years—a tragic Civil War, women's suffrage and a wrenching Civil Rights struggle—before full rights of citizenship would be legally guaranteed for all citizens.

The economic roots of a second American revolution can be traced to *The Wealth of Nations*, written in 1776 by a Scot,

Adam Smith. He stated, "The skill, dexterity and knowledge of a nation's people is the most powerful engine of its economic growth."[51] In the early 1800s, a struggle began between the agrarian slave-labor economy of the South and the industrial manufacturing economy of the North. After the Civil War, the Industrial Revolution accelerated. By the middle of the 20th century, America's economic progress reflected the vision, commitment, savings, investment, and skill of its citizens. America became a "melting pot" of immigrants and their children searching for the American dream of economic prosperity. In 1911, for example, one in ten African Americans was classified as middle class; in 1950, one in six and by 1967 two of three.[52] During this time, most other Americans emerged from poverty to share a middle-class standard of living enjoyed by only a fraction of the world's population.

Since the 1980s, however, the poverty level among all Americans has increased, from a low of 11 percent to about 15 percent. Poverty now claims 36 million citizens, with 42 percent living in decaying, terror-filled cities. One in every five children is poor. Poverty now costs the nation $230 billion annually in lost revenue; and the consequences of our neglect are building.[53]

In April 1992, the world watched the sixth-worst disaster in modern American history. Television recorded 72 hours of burning, looting, assaults and murder in South Central Los Angeles by Caucasian, African, Mexican and Asian Americans. By the time the smoke had cleared, 51 people were dead and 2,383 were injured. More than 5,200 buildings were severely damaged or destroyed. An estimated 17,000 people were arrested and 40,000 jobs were lost.

The tragedy of Los Angeles illustrates the bankruptcy of our national values relating to education and job training for our urban poor. But the cancer of ignorance is not limited to our cities. It spreads like an epidemic throughout our nation and will impact all citizens.

The only escape for Americans held hostage by ignorance is through disciplined character development and competitive knowledge gained from a quality education. Public educators alone cannot fight and win our war against ignorance. Parents, senior citizens and other community volunteers can help teachers empower the public schools. Building responsible learning cultures simply requires a commitment of focused time and energy.

Quality education requires that each American recognize: *First,* knowledge is the most valuable capital in today's global economy. *Second,* our cultural devaluation of public education for all Americans is making the United States economically uncompetitive. *Third,* to become competitive again, we must declare war against ignorance. *Fourth,* we must participate in a knowledge network and complete Learning Improvement Contracts. *Fifth,* we must create responsible learning cultures in every organization to which we belong—family, school, business, media, community and government. *Sixth,* for our increased investment of scarce resources in public schools, we must demand world-class student academic performance. *Victory demands that we start a Knowledge Revolution before it's too late for ourselves, our children and our grandchildren.*

APPENDICES

Knowledge Revolution Quiz for All Americans

Please circle the correct answer

1. What percentage of American goods/services now have competitors in the global knowledge economy?

   a. 80% b. 60% c. 40%

2. What percentage of Americans now have jobs related to the information/knowledge economy?

   a. 30% b. 42% c. 58%

3. Compared to the 12 leading nations of the world, where does the U.S. rank in educational achievement of high school students?

   a. bottom b. top c. middle

4. On average, how much has each person in America lost in income since 1973 because of America's slow economic growth?

   a. $5,000 b. $17,000 c. $28,000

5. In the culture of immediate gratification, the media exploit:

   a. children b. adolescents
   c. adults d. everyone

6. On average, how many hours each week do American children watch TV?

   a. 30 hrs. b. 20 hrs. c. 10 hrs.

7. Non-competitive Americans are:

   a. unhealthy b. uneducated
   c. low-skilled d. all

8. Civilian entitlements and defense spending together account for what percent of the federal budget?

   a. 33% b. 56% c. 74%

9. A successful democratic civic culture depends on an implied contract between citizens who are:

a. accountable b. educated
c. fairly taxed d. all

10. Prospering cultures value:

a. work b. education c. savings
d. family e. community f. all

11. Leadership to build responsible learning cultures depends on:

a. luck b. natural talent
c. commitment and training d. love only

12. Parents should teach their children:

a. personal discipline b. work
c. responsibility d. all of these

13. Public educators should teach children:

a. basic leadership skills
b. responsibility to self, family and community
c. world-class knowledge
d. all

14. Higher educators should train teachers in:

a. teaching effectively
b. meeting world-class standards of knowledge
c. assessing skills
d. managing schools and classrooms
e. conducting research
f. all

15. Community leaders can help public schools by:

a. criticizing b. doing their own thing
c. replacing them d. building partnerships

16. The proportion of corporate education grants contributed to public schools is:

a. 50% b. 6% c. 30%

17. This year's interest on the federal debt ($300 billion) is about what percentage of the total cost of public schooling in America:

a. 75% b. 133% c. 25%

18. Additional federal "high performance investment" in education reform should result in increased:

a. salaries
b. buildings
c. student achievement

19. "Relevant Knowledge" requires:

a. accurate information b. useful value framework
c. skillful application d. all

20. The Third American Revolution requires leadership to bring about a major cultural transformation that is being driven by:

a. politics b. knowledge c. economics

21. Bonus: Name your Member of Congress _______________

____

Sample Learning Improvement Contract (LIC)

Date:

This LIC is between ___(parent)_____ and ___(teacher/ school official)____on behalf of ____(student)_________ who is enrolled in ____(school)_________.

Parental Responsibilities

1. Parent(s) will help the child develop a positive attitude about school. They will ensure that the child arrives at school prepared for the day's learning activities, follows school rules, carries out teachers' instructions and directions, and works diligently to master information and skills.

2. Parent(s) will ensure that _______(student)_____attends school regularly, is on time each day, and misses school only when absolutely necessary.

3. Parent(s) will help safeguard the health and physical strength of _____(student)_____ so that he/she will have adequate nourishment and rest to face the rigors of school activities each day.

4. Parent(s) will support the school work activities of _____(student)_____ by encouraging homework completion, setting aside study time at home, creating an atmosphere for learning, and monitoring the child's homework assignments to see that the child completes them on time.

5. Parent(s) will keep in touch with ____(student's)____ teacher(s) by regularly responding to messages and reports from school, attending parent/teacher conferences, discussing with the child in detail the report card or other measures of achievement, and conferring with both child and teacher on how the parent(s) can help the child improve in areas needing attention.

This sample is a revision of the Memorandum of Understanding from Terrel H. Bell and Donna L. Elmquist, *How to Shape Up Our Nation's Schools: Three Crucial Steps for American Education* (1991). In some circumstances, "guardian(s)" or "mentor(s)" may be more appropriate than "parent(s)," depending upon who has responsibility for the student.

6. Parent(s) will prepare ___(student)___ for school events such as examinations and other activities by providing extra rest and support prior to the event or exam, praising and recognizing good work, discussing both strong and weak points and planning a course of action at home for even better performance.

7. Parent(s) will facilitate ___(student's)___ completion of the school district's specified reading requirements for advancing to the next school grade by discussing and supervising their child's reading activities early and continuously throughout the school year. Parent(s) will assume responsibility for the child's meeting these requirements.

School Responsibilities

1. (Student's)___ teacher and other school personnel will welcome ___(student's)___ parent(s) to participate in an effective parent-school partnership on behalf of the child. Educators will be supportive in offering suggestions to help parent(s) accomplish the responsibilities outlined above.

2. School personnel will strive to keep ___(student's)___ parent(s) informed of special school events affecting the child. The school calendar and notices will be sent home regularly so parent(s) will know of examinations, deadlines and dates of parent-teacher conferences and other activities.

3. School personnel will keep ___(student's)___ parent(s) informed about progress in meeting school achievement requirements, as well as problems that will require special parental attention. School personnel will notify parents promptly of absences, tardiness, incomplete homework, incomplete school work, and breaking school rules.

4. School personnel will respond in a timely manner to parental requests for information about ___(student)___ progress at school or about problems that parents may perceive.

5. School personnel will provide textbooks, supplies, and other materials necessary for school progress (within the limits of school budget restrictions beyond the school's control). School personnel will offer special assistance to students or parents who need it.

6. School personnel will implement the school district's

6. School personnel will implement the school district's required reading program by meeting with parents, informing them of their responsibilities, and discussing the program in detail. The mandatory and optional reading lists will be provided early in the school year so that (student) may begin early in the year to meet these requirements. School personnel will check on the availability of listed books at local and school libraries and will notify the school district office of any book shortages.

7. School personnel will compile and provide a list of approved volunteer reading counselors along with their phone numbers and addresses. School personnel will also provide (student) with a reading "pass off" card to be presented to reading counselors to sign when a reading requirement has been met.

This sample LIC promotes understanding and cooperation between us—(student's) parent(s) and school personnel. By clarifying mutual and separate responsibilities and expectations, we can better teach and motivate (student) to have an educationally productive school year. By working together, we can enhance the child's education by providing effective support at home and at school. Although this is not a legally binding contract enforceable in a court of law, we publicly make these commitments to facilitate the child's development and preparation for productive, satisfying citizenship.

Student ______________________ Date ______________

Parent ______________________ Date ______________

School Official __________________ Date ______________

For additional information on how to design your personal Learning Partner LIC, call the Knowledge Network at 1-800-736-4877, (#4008).

FEDERAL EDUCATION AND TRAINING PROGRAMS

In 1992 the following federal education programs impact virtually every public school district in the United States. Higher education programs for teacher and administrator training and development, research and financial aid also benefit K–12 schools.

Head Start for disadvantaged preschool students is funded at $2.2 billion, but serves 28 percent of eligible children.

Elementary and Secondary Education—Chapter 1 funds of $6.7 billion are distributed to virtually every school district. **Chapter 2** is funded at nearly $500 million.

Special Education is funded at $2.9 billion.

Bilingual Education and Minority Language Affairs is funded at $225 million.

Native American Education is funded at approximately $1 billion.

TRIO programs, such as Upward Bound, are funded at $385 million.

The Office of Civil Rights is funded at $54 million.

Department of Defense Overseas Dependents Schools is funded at $904 million.

Educational Research and Improvement and Assessment Programs are funded at $268 million plus $148 million for libraries.

Science Education is funded at $1.9 billion.

The National Endowments for the Arts and Humanities Education Programs include $7.6 million for arts education, and most of the $176 million humanities budget impacts education.

Vocational Education is funded at $1 billion.

Youth Retraining for economically disadvantaged youth (JTPA) is funded at $4 billion.

For a comprehensive analysis of federal education programs see: Lloyd, et al., *Knowledge Revolution for All Americans: Competing in Our Global Economy* (in press, 1993).

NOTES ON METHODOLOGY

Knowledge for All Americans: Winning the War Against Ignorance—Empowering Public Schools, was written by Kent Lloyd, Diane Ramsey, and Sven Groennings, who take full responsibility for its contents. Jack Carlson was the special contributor on investment strategies. Scot Hymas made significant contributions to the final report. Twenty outside experts also contributed to the report. Center corporate and foundation sponsors, outside readers and other supporters are not responsible for the findings or recommendations of this report. Lenora Cox, Carolyn and Eric Miller, Samantha O'Neill and Rebecca Dean Shipp were research and editorial assistants. Dixie T. Barlow was editorial and production consultant. Morris Musig designed the cover and Better Impressions of Reston, Virginia printed the booklet.

Experts who read the text were Dr. Terrel Bell, John Bowman, Mary L. Bradford, Wayne Burnette, Christopher Cross, Bruce Christensen, Dr. Ramon Cortines, Dr. Stuart Gothold, Hon. Augustus F. Hawkins, Dr. Floretta McKenzie, Ladd McNamara, M.D., Kathie Nielsen, Dr. Kendall O. Price, Dr. Susan Solomon Scribner and Thomas Shannon.

Policy research for this report focusing on public school reform was taken in large part from *Knowledge Revolution for All Americans: Competing in Our Global Economy* (in press, 1993). The study was conducted by Kent Lloyd, Ph.D., Sven Groennings, Ph.D., Diane Ramsey, Ph.D. and Jack Carlson, Ph.D., of the Knowledge for All Americans Center, along with 130 expert consultants, panelists and editors. The five-year study presents a comprehensive strategy for improving American competitiveness from early-childhood education through workforce retraining. It proposes new approaches and practical revisions in the 18 major federal program areas which together command the world's largest education and training budget. It offers more than 200 recommendations. The larger policy study is the first comprehensive resource document on federal education and training programs. More broadly, it provides an integrated framework for reform in our nation's education and training systems.

KNOWLEDGE FOR ALL AMERICANS CENTER NATIONAL ADVISORY COMMITTEE

CHAIRS

Hon. Terrel H. Bell, former U.S. Secretary of Education

Hon. Augustus F. Hawkins, former Chairman, House Education & Labor Committee

Hon. C. William Verity, former U.S. Secretary of Commerce

VICE CHAIRS

Nolan Archibald, Chairman, President & CEO, Black & Decker Corporation

Bruce Christensen, President & CEO, Public Broadcasting Service

C. Emily Feistritzer, Publisher, *Education Reports*

MEMBERS

Hon. V.J. Adduci, Chairman, Innovative Technologies, Inc.; American Automotive International

Hon. Edward Aguirre, President, Aguirre International; former U.S. Commissioner of Education

G. Carl Ball, Chairman of the Board, George J. Ball, Inc.

Thomas C. Boysen, Kentucky Commissioner of Education

W. Hughes Brockbank, Chairman, Pine Mountain Corporation

Johnnetta B. Cole, President, Spelman College

Ramon C. Cortines, former Superintendent, San Francisco Public Schools

John P. Crecine, President, Georgia Institute of Technology

Hon. Christopher T. Cross, Education Director, Business Roundtable

Fred C. Davison, President, National Science Center Foundation

Robert C. Dockson, Chairman-Emeritus, CalFed, Inc.

Morris Gordon, Chairman of Education, Washington, D.C. Board of Rabbis

Stuart E. Gothold, Superintendent, Los Angeles County Public Schools

John C. Hoy, President, New England Board of Higher Education

Floretta McKenzie, former Superintendent of Schools, Washington, D.C.

Robert W. Mendenhall, President & CEO, Wicat Systems

Hon. Ronald Packard, Congressman (R-CA), House Science & Technology Committee

Kendall O. Price, President, Center for Leadership Development

Hon. Joel Pritchard, Lieutenant Governor, State of Washington

Hon. Peter Smith, Dean, School of Education and Human Development, George Washington University

Arthur R. Taylor, Dean, Graduate School of Business Administration, Fordham University

Howard E. Wall, President, Post-Newsweek Cable

Phillip L. Williams, Vice Chairman, Times Mirror Company; Chair, California Chamber of Commerce Education Committee

Hon. Andrew Young, former Mayor, City of Atlanta

Georges Karam, Financial Adviser

SPONSORS AND CONTRIBUTORS

Corporate Partners

Ahmanson Foundation
American Express Foundation
ARCO Foundation
AT&T Foundation
Hughes Aircraft Company
Novell, Inc.
Pfizer Foundation

Corporate Associates

Foundation for Financial Education
Geneva Steel Company
Jenner & Block
Karamco, Inc.
Packard Foundation
Pine Mountain Corporation
Public Broadcasting Service
Rockwell International
WICAT Systems

Corporate Affiliates

Aguirre International
Ball Foundation
Basic Foods
Better Impressions
Black & Decker
Cal Fed, Inc.
Cannon Industries
John Shooshan Co.
Marina Ventures
Mason Properties
Post-Newsweek Cable
Security Pacific Foundation
Times Mirror Co.
Whittaker Corporation

Individual Contributors

Hon. V.J. and Kathleen B. Adduci
Dr. John T. and Linda Alexander
Lori Annaheim
Temple Ashbrook II and
Loretta Hyatt-Ashbrook
Dixie and Allan Barlow
John and Tyra Behrens
John and Margaret Bowman
Mary L. Bradford
Scott Bradford
Wayne M. and Dorothy Burnette
Hon. Kent and Winnie Burton
Jack and Renee Carlson
Douglas A. Clark
Dr. Ramon Cortines
Lenora Cox
Dr. Kent and Janice Christensen
Hon. Christopher T. Cross
Arthur Dee and
Catherine Barbara Decker
Francis and Pauline Eichbush
Dr. C. Emily Feistritzer and
Paul Mertens
Dr. Morris and Lori Gordon
Dr. Stuart E. Gothold
Pamela Greene
Suzanne Groennings
David and Leslie Guido
Ronald D. Harmon
Kristin Hartt
Hon. Augustus F. Hawkins
Hon. Allan and Irmina Howe
Jerry and Edith Hymas
Scot and Jeralie Hymas
Dr. Sar Levitan
Ann Kappler and Brent Rushforth
Dr. Gary and Donna Lloyd
Georges, Mia and Christina Karam
Mark Kurson
Zane and Louise Mason
Dr. Ladd and Susan McNamara
David and Carrie Miller
Carolyn and Eric Miller
Dr. Thomas F. and Heidi Mosher
Morris and Lynne Musig
Will Newman and Joyce Dunnigan
Kathie and Peter Nielson
Samantha L. O'Neill
Barbara G. Perch
David and Kellie Persinger
Dr. Kendall O. and Dr. Deon Price
Shep Ranbohm
Lewis and Evelyn Ramsey
Steven and Christine Ramsey
Virginia C. Riedy
Dr. Susan Solomon Scribner
Dr. Royal Shipp
Rebecca Dean Shipp
Boyd and Jill Smith
Carl and Donna Snow
John Shooshan
Dr. Wendell M. and Monetta Smoot
Rudi S. Southerland
Dwayne and Carolyn Stevenson
Jennifer Tepper
Thomas Toch

STUDY REFERENCES

1. Kent Lloyd, Sven Groennings, Diane Ramsey, Jack Carlson, *Knowledge Revolution for All Americans: Competing in Our Global Economy* (in press, 1993).
2. Ibid.
3. Education Commission of the States' Information Clearing House, January 1991.
4. Lawrence Mishel and Jared Bernstein of the Economic Policy Institute, *The State of Working in America* (1992).
5. James Madison, "No. 10," *The Federalist Papers*, Clinton Rossiter, ed. (1961).
6. David P. Calleo, *The Bankrupting of America: How the Federal Budget is Impoverishing the Nation* (1992).
7. *Northwest Ordinance of l787.*
8. David A. Hamburg, *Today's Children: Creating a Future for a Generation in Crisis* (1992).
9. Robert B. Reich, *The Work of Nations: Preparing Ourselves for 21st Century Capitalism* (1991).
10. The National Commission on Children, *Beyond Rhetoric: A New American Agenda for Children and Families* (1991).
11. Children's Defense Fund, *Leave No Children Behind* (1991).
12. *Fortune*, 10 August 1992; see also 1991 Health and Human Services Report, *The Washington Post*, 12 September 1991.
13. Juliet B. Schor, *The Overworked American: The Unexpected Decline of Leisure* (1991).
14. Terrel H. Bell and Donna L. Elmquist, *How to Shape Up Our Nation's Schools* (1991); see also Dorothy Rich, *MEGASKILLS: How Families Can Help Children Succeed in School and Beyond* (1988).
15. International Association for the Evaluation of Educational Achievement, *Science Achievement in Seventeen Countries: A Preliminary Report* (1988).
16. Selected key references on excellent or healthy families include: Nathan Caplan, Marcella H. Choy, and John K. Whitmore, "Indochinese Refugee Families and Academic Achievement," *Scientific American*, February 1992; Dolores Curran, *Traits of a*

Healthy Family (1983); Ray Guarendi, *Back to the Family* (1990); Nick Stinnett and John DeFrain, *Secrets of Strong Families* (1985).

17. James B. Twitchell, *Carnival Culture: The Trashing of Taste in America* (1992); Deborah Baldwin, "The Hard Sell," *The Utne Reader*, January/February 1992.
18. Andrew L. Shapiro, *We're Number One: Where America Stands and Falls in the New World Order* (1992); *Fortune*, 10 August 1992.
19. Economic Policy Institute, *The State of America's Children 1991* (1991).
20. Tipper Gore, *Raising PG Kids in an X-Rated Society* (1987).
21. *The Washington Post*, 28 July 1992.
22. Brendon S. Centerwell, "Television and Violence," *Journal of American Medical Association*, vol. 267, no. 22, (1992).
23. Michael Wolff, Peter Rutten, Albert F. Bayers III, and the World Rank Research Team, *Where We Stand: Can America Make It in the Global Race for Wealth, Health, and Happiness?* (1992).
24. George R. Kaplan, *Images of Education: The Mass Media's Version of America's Schools* (1992).

25 Harris Poll, 1991. The Harris Education Research Center, *An Assessment of American Education: The View of Employers, Higher Educators, the Public, Recent Students and their Parents*, (September 1991), sponsored by the Council on Economic Development and The Business Roundtable.

26. Center for Civic Education and the Council for the Advancement of Citizenship, *Civitas: A Framework for Civic Education*, (1991); see work of Jefferson Center for Character Education.
27. Martin Haberman, "The Pedagogy of Poverty Versus Good Teaching," *Phi Delta Kappan*, December 1991.
28. Jonathan Kozol, *Savage Inequalities* (1991).
29. U.S. Department of Education, Office of Educational Research and Improvement, National Center for Education Statistics, *The Condition of Education 1992* (1992).
30. Lloyd, et al., *Knowledge Revolution for All Americans: Competing in Our Global Economy.*
31. Derek Bok, *Universities and the Future of America* (1990).

32. Arthur M. Schlesinger, Jr., *The Disuniting of America: Reflections on a Multicultural Society* (1991).

33. "EXXCEL Links Home With the School," *Los Angeles Times*, 22 June 1992.

34. Peter F. Drucker, *Managing the Non-Profit Organization: Principles and Practices,* (1990); "Profiting from Non-Profits," *BusinessWeek*, 26 March 1990.

35. National Research Council, *A Common Destiny: Blacks and American Society* (1989); Eric Lincoln and Lawrence H. Mamiya, *The Black Church and the African American Experience* (1990).

36. Eugene H. Methvin, "The Stuff of Champions," *Reader's Digest,* October 1991.

37. *America 2000: An Education Strategy* (1991).

38. National Research Council, *Research and Education Reform: Roles for the Office of Educational Research and Improvement* (1992).

39. "The 24th Annual Gallup/Phi Delta Kappan Poll of the Public's Attitudes Toward the Public Schools," *Phi Delta Kappan,* September 1992.

40. Lloyd, et al., *Knowledge Revolution for All Americans: Competing in Our Global Economy.*

41. Lester Thurow, *Head to Head* (1992).

42. U.S. Department of Labor, *Economic Change and the American Workforce* (1992).

43. For an analysis, see William J. Baumol, Sue Anne Batey Blackman, and Edward N. Wolff, *Productivity and American Leadership: The Long View* (1989).

44. These 1989 figures were taken from the National Center for Education Statistics, *The Condition of Education 1992* (1992). U.S. data include unusually high expenditures ($13,600 average per student) for "special education" students, who are 10.6 percent of all public school students. These high expenditures mask lower funding for regular students. For an analysis showing the U.S. near the bottom of industrial nations in the percentage of GDP spent on public schools see M. Edith Rasell and Lawrence Mishel of the Economic Policy Institute, *Shortchanging Educa-*

tion: How U.S. Spending on Grades K-12 Lags Behind Other Industrial Nations (1990) and *Measuring Comparative Education Spending: A Response to the Department of Education* (1990).

45. Lawrence E. Harrison, *Who Prospers? How Cultural Values Shape Economic and Political Success* (1992).

46. Warren Bennis, *On Becoming a Leader,* (1989); John W. Gardner, *On Leadership,* (1990); Edgar H. Schein, *Organizational Culture and Leadership* (1985); Steven Covey, *The Seven Habits for Effective People: Powerful Lessons in Personal Change* (1990).

47. For further discussion on the crisis facing our children see, Hamburg, *Today's Children, Creating a Future for a Generation in Crisis* (1992); William J. Bennett, *The Devaluing of America: The Fight for Our Culture and Our Children* (1992).

48. Bell, et al., *How to Shape Up Our Nation's Schools.*

49. A. J. Ayer, *Thomas Paine,* Daniel Edwin Wheeler, ed., *Common Sense; The Crisis; Life and Writings of Thomas Paine* (1908).

50. Clinton Rossiter, ed., *The Federalist Papers* (1961); Catherine Drinker Bowen, *Miracle At Philadelphia: The Story of the Constitutional Convention May to September, 1787* (1966).

51. Adam Smith, *An Inquiry into the Causes of the Nature and Wealth of Nations* (1776; 1837); see also Max Weber, *The Protestant Ethic and the Spirit of Capitalism* (1904; 1930).

52. Harrison, *Who Prospers? How Cultural Values Shape Economic and Political Success.*

53. "The Economic Crisis of Urban America," *BusinessWeek*, 18 May 1992.

HIEBERT LIBRARY
3 6877 00189 7635

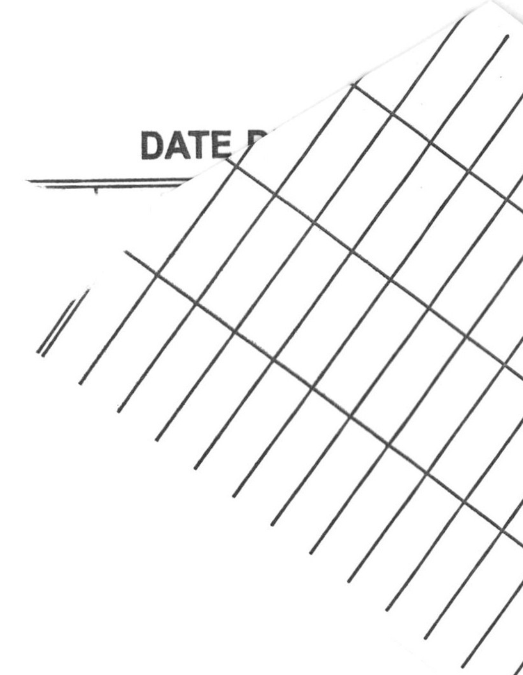
DATE D